Dogs don't know Kung fu

A female guide to Self Protection

By

Jamie O'Keefe

Photos taken by J.O'Keefe & Bob Peters
Thanks to Micky Bennett for appearing in photos
Photographs scanned by
KTP Printers
Unit 37G
Princelet Street
London E1 5LP
Tel: 0171 247 0786

Copyright Jamie O'Keefe 1996

Published by

New Breed publishing

A CIP catalogue record for this book is available from the British Library

Printed and bound in Great Britain.

ISBN 0 9517567 1 0

Please note: The theoretical information and physical techniques outlined in this book are for self Protection and Self defence purposes only. The author and the publishers cannot accept any responsibility for any proceedings or prosecutions brought or instituted against any person or body as a result of the misuse of any theoretical information or physical techniques described in this book or any loss, injury or damage caused thereby.

Dedicated to

my Mother , Sister, and all who have

suffered in silence

Acknowledgements

Thanks to:-

Pete West for proof reading, honest criticism and help in turning this book from a dream into reality.

Kevin Raymond & Gavin at KTP Printers.

Geoff Thompsom for being a friend outside of the Martial arts when I was suffering in silence.

Peter Consterdine for his support, help and professionalism when I needed it most within my teaching.

DaveTourton for the short stick training and being everything that I ever respected and still do within the martial arts.

My friends and critics within the New Breed Self Protection system for being themselves.

Pete & Tracy Chamberlain for true friendship.

Marion East, Christine Lloyd, Dorothy Davis, Margaret Harriot, and the girls for having faith in my female self protection courses.

Geoff Britton and Liz (Magpie) for giving me my first two girls schools and for always being there if needed.

My mother who I love dearly, and my children, Jamie, Ricky, Adam & Kirsty who make my whole life worthwhile.

Sophie, for making my heart smile.....

Foreword

I'm not usually known for writing forewords to books on self protection, and not because I'm afraid of competition, on the contrary, the more people offering good advice in the fight for better protection the better:- rather its because most of what I read on the subject is crap.

I would never be happy putting my name to something that does not represent my own views, and that's putting it mildly. Not only are the proffered 'self defence' techniques in these manuals unlikely, they are also, very often, dangerous and opinionated.

I have written some 20 books to date on self protection and related subject's so you'd think that there would be very little left for me to learn. I rarely if ever find a manuscript that inspires me or even one that offers something new, a fresh perspective, an innovative approach.

Jamie's book did all the latter. He offered inspiration and sensible (and in retrospect, obvious) solutions to the many enigmatic 'grey areas' that had long perplexed me, a so called expert.

Questions that I have been pondering upon for years were answered at the first reading of this text. So I not only commend Mr O'Keefe on writing probably the best self protection book for women on the market but I also thank him for filling in the gaps in what is, at best, a very intangible subject.

What makes this book even more unique is that Jamie is a veteran instructor with thousands of hours of women's self protection under his belt, he is also an empiricist in that he has put his training to work in real life situations.

Now while this may not say a lot to the lay man/woman, to those in the know, it speaks volumes.

Most of the instructors out there teaching self protection have never been in a real situation and so garnish unreal scenarios with un-workable, hypothetical technique.
You will get no such balderdash from this cutting edge instructor. What is offered on the menu in this text will prepare you, of that I have no doubt.

Self protection in the very violent 20th century must now, out of necessity be viewed as an environmental seat belt, it can no longer be down graded as a recreational pastime that comes third down the list of priorities after basket weaving, people are being attacked and killed, every day of the week, in un-provoked, un-solicited and bloody attacks.

My advice to you the reader is to take on board what Jamie has to offer as preventive measures and make them part of your life. Being aware will help you to avoid the majority of attack scenarios, for those that fall outside the periphery of avoidance, the simple, yet effective physical techniques on offer in this book will, if employed with conviction, help to neutralise even the most ardent of attackers.

This is a great book that makes great sense.

The best of its kind.

Geoff Thompson. Coventry 1996

Introduction

Over the last 20 years I have spent an awful lot of my time in Martial arts training halls and clubs learning how to better protect myself, and other close to me against society's violent minority. Initially my efforts were in vain and I often ended up, rather painfully, on the receiving end of an attackers fist or boot with my 'Self defence' strategies - I use the term loosely - and ego shattered like porcelain on the pavement.
Rather than be put off by my early mistakes, like so many before me, I struggled onwards in a bid to learn as much about 'real' self defence, the kind that doesn't shatter under pressure, as I could.

My search became a matter of survival and led to a lifetime study and systematic analysis of the Martial arts.

I learned many things along the way, not least of which was that much of what was being sold under the guise of self defence was of no use in a brutal arena-the street- that often punished failure with death.

After two decades of pressure testing my heard earned knowledge, I devised my own method of self protection courses which I teach throughout the UK adapting my teaching methods according to the needs of the individual groups.

One of the areas that has rapidly gained my interest in this time is that of Self protection for Women. This. I felt, was where the 'Grey areas' seemed in abundance.

To this end I now spend the greatest proportion of my time concentrating on teaching self protection to school girls from the age of 11, through to the 6th form, moving onto specialised courses for adult females.

Many will be surprised by the advice on offer in this book, others who have placed blind faith in their hard earned Martial arts belts and grades may even be shocked, But that's OK, a good shock is often better than good advice.

I should know, I went from being a bullied child to achieving my 4th Dan black belt in Karate in my search for the 'secrets' of self defence, only to find out that the only secret was - and it was very well kept- **there were no secrets**.

Although I was able to kick, punch, throw, and perform techniques that awed the average person, there was still something amiss!

The so called secret that was missing from my Martial arts curriculum was what many people ostentatiously refer to as the 6th sense, or what I like to refer to as *' Common-sense'*.

Not only did a small amount of common sense change my own training methods and selection of techniques for the better but it also led me to where I am at this moment in time, teaching self protection for women that works.

What started this sudden change of direction and triggered the forementioned 'common sense' was the birth of my daughter Kirsty, who is now five years old.

Which, I asked myself, out of all the information, skills and techniques I had so arduously and proudly collated over a lifetime of training would I see fit to pass on to her?

Would my library and database of defence techniques pull my own daughter from the jaws of attack should she ever become 'another victim'?

Working as a doorman in some pretty rough places there are times when you seriously wonder whether you will see the next day.

I'd watched so called 'experts' throw superfluous techniques into the mincer of a real situation only to get chewed up and spat back out again. I had seen big men fail to successfully employ many of the techniques that I held in my artillery and I knew that I had to give my daughter what I considered essential technique and information for her survival. So I started my search for the grail of truth.

As there was little of any real value which catered for female self protection, I decided to write my findings in a book so that it would not only help to serve the females in my own family but all females,

Please do not be misled into thinking that you can protect yourself by acquiring the coveted black belt, I can tell you now that a belt is no guarantee of anything.

If you are unfortunate enough to experience a physical attack, the odds will be stacked heavily against you. However, if you invest just a little time studying this book, and put into practice the lessons taught, you will go a long way to protecting yourself and your loved ones.

Who are we afraid of?

Who's afraid of the big bad wolf, the big bad wolf, the big bad, wolf?

We are all afraid of the big, bad, wolf! So, who is the big, bad, wolf? We all have a different Big Bad Wolf to fear. Unfortunately for women, the fear is far more justified.

The Big Bad Wolf is Man and he tends to treat his fellow man rather differently to women!

Generally, Man does not have to fear attack from females, being sexually assaulted or raped by a female, becoming pregnant, losing his virginity unwillingly or being subjected to sexual assaults from women.

He does not generally need to fear being raped by another man, unless placed in abnormal circumstances, like prison or other such institutions where heterosexual relationships are not possible. Men only fear each other on the level of non-sexual violence. This is the reason why every martial art club is packed out with men. Sadly, many men appear to enjoy violence and long for the opportunity to wallow in it, if not on the football terraces, then on the battle-field.

Females are different. Realistically women need have little fear of each other with regard to physical violence. Neither need they fear other women jumping out from behind bushes to rape them, getting them pregnant, infecting them with the Aids virus or of performing an act of gross indecency against them.

For Woman there is only one Big Bad Wolf, namely Man and his abuse of Power and control over women..

It is due to the Big Bad Wolf out there that I am writing this book.

I am ashamed to be associated with the abusers and rapists who unfortunately share my gender.

As a man I realise that every single day in the street many women will pass me by and sadly feel intimidated. They will have been frightened by the deserved reputation of Man. However, fortunately, we are not all the same.

I have a mother, a sister, a niece and a beautiful daughter and care for their safety in this sad world. Most right minded men are the same. It is only the small minority of men in our midst who do not care for women. It is these who are the dangerous ones. For them, women are fruit to be taken at will. Flesh to be eaten. It is they who choose to take power and control of another body.

The most difficult problem is how to tell the difference between everyday man and the Big Bad Wolf. In many cases this is not possible until it is too late. However, with a little information and training you can take great strides in self protection.

This is the aim of my book. I must make it quite clear, who it is that we fear because we will be basing our studies, information and training around the threat that exists.

If you are serious about raising your awareness with regards your personal survival and self protection, please read on.

Forget learning how to score points in a Martial Arts club. Forget trying to win trophies in Martial Arts contests. Forget relying on others to protect you. **WAKE UP!** If you do not, the Big Bad Wolf may decide to play out his little power game with you in a starring role.

Yes, it can happen to **<u>YOU</u>**. No audition will be required. You will only need to fit a simple criteria.

Firstly, you have to be a female. Any colour, race or creed, age or physical appearance will do, he will not discriminate. Secondly, you will need to be unaware and switched off.

Do you feel lucky? No? Good! Let's not make his day.

I want to teach you how to take care of yourself. Together, we can beat this low-life. We should set him along the path of <u>extinction</u>.

Rape - does it happen?

In the real world how many women have actually witnessed a rape? How many women have been raped?
The answer to both of these questions is that the majority have not. Compared to our chance of being seriously hurt in a car smash or having our handbags snatched, the chances of us being raped are far less. So how do we know rape is for real? The answer, of course, is through the media and through stories told second-hand.

 Rapes are regularly reported in magazines, Daily Papers, Radio and Television. It is the media we have to thank for bringing the ugliness of rape to our attention.

Consider what would have happened if the Aids Virus had never been reported.
Many more people would have become infected through ignorance.
In the case of rape we seem to hear of cases all of the time. In fact, we hear so much about it that we start to imagine that it is happening all around us yet somehow we still become desensitised to it.

However, the sad truth is that rape occurs far more than it is ever reported. For all sorts of personal reasons many women never report cases of rape. Some may live in fear of further harm from their attacker if they report him. Some feel they will not be taken seriously. Others fear they may be branded slag's. Some women fear the rape may lead to their being rejected by their husbands or partners.
Sadly, many rapists will not get reported because they are close relatives or friends of the victims.
Many women are forced to have unwanted sex within a marriage and never realise that this is also rape.
We must take notice of the rape cases reported in the media.
Some brave victim has not only just experienced a horrific ordeal, she has also had the guts to report it. She has gone through the motions of getting a monster chained, to protect others.

She has taken away his power and control and put him on the receiving end of the laws application of power and control.

Rape victims are our main source of information on real rape encounters. Without them sharing this information, of their suffering with us, we would have nothing.

The more rapist that do not get exposed and dealt with, the more female society are going to suffer. We must watch and listen to these stories and learn. Gradually it will sink in and we will open our eyes to the truth. It can happen to us too.

Any female can become the next victim. As long as we do not become paranoid hermits, this type of thinking is good.

We have to learn to **stay switched on.**

Read into the ugliness of the ordeal these women have suffered and try to put yourself in their place. How would you have coped? Be real! It could happen to you.

Lets learn to do something positive because Prevention is better than the cure!.

Rape - the possibilities

⇒ MALE RAPING FEMALE   MALE RAPING MALE
⇒ FEMALE RAPING MALE   FEMALE RAPING FEMALE

So, we know full well that Rape happens. We will now look at some of the possibilities.

MALE RAPING FEMALE.
This is the most common and main subject of my book, so I will not deal with it here.

MALE RAPING MALE.
This type of rape seems to be making an appearance in the news. It was only recently reported that a number of such attacks had occurred on the Underground network in London. A recent T.V. programme suggested that male rape is on the increase and that the attacks are extremely violent. However, most men do not walk the streets in fear of such attacks.

One place where the fear will be more prevalent for men is in institutions. Whether he be straight or gay, a man sent to prison or other such establishments will be on his guard. Young men and boys have also been the victims of rape in children's homes, remand centres, boarding schools, etc.
 The Aids virus is very easily passed on in this type of rape if the attacker's penis is pushed into the victim's anus (bum). In so doing the victim's skin can be torn, thereby allowing the mixing of bodily fluids (sperm and blood).
Oral sex, meaning that the attacker places his penis in the victim's mouth or visa versa may also occur during male rape. This may remove the physical pain of forced anal sex, but may still involve a risk of Aids transmission as a result of the attacker's sperm getting into the victim's mouth.

Another act that may be involved is when the victim is forced to push his tongue in and out of the attacker's anus. This is known as "rimming". One of the nastiest acts is known as "fist-up". This is a procedure whereby the attacker attempts to push his hand and arm, as far as possible, into the victim's anus.

Now, I hope I have shocked you, not because I take any pleasure from shocking, but because I want to alert you to the real world. What these unfortunate male victims have been forced to endure, women also have to suffer **AND MUCH MORE**.

Forget the illusion that rape may only be an unpleasant straight, lay. I want to alert you to the real facts.

FEMALE RAPING MALE.

This is very rare. Sometimes it is pulled out of the hat when a man is caught having an affair.

FEMALE RAPING FEMALE

On the streets this seems to be unknown. Problems may occur in institutions but generally there is little real danger.

The Sexual Offences Act 1956 simply declared *that*

" It is an offence for a man to rape a woman "

However this was not defined clearly and needed to be further amended in 1976 to state that a man commits rape if

" he has unlawful sexual intercourse with a woman who at the time of the intercourse does not consent to it; and at the time he knows that she does not consent to the intercourse or he is reckless as to whether she consents to it"

Butterworths Police Law 1994

Scream as loud as you can!
(if he let's you)

The first thing that we do when we feel pain is to make a noise. We do not plan it, we have not been taught it. It is a natural response. The same applies to screaming, which we do whenever we are scared.

Women are usually able to deliver a real strong, high pitched scream that is guaranteed to attract attention. Do you really think, that your attacker is going to want you to tell everybody within earshot, that he is about to rape you? I do not think so! This is actually the first priority the rapist has. Shut the victim up. His power and control of you begins.

Manual strangulation, sometimes called throttling, will often result in death. This occurs when an attacker uses excessive pressure to stop a panicking victim from screaming. I will explain this more in the section entitled:- **The neck is your Lifeline**.

If you apply light pressure with only one hand to your throat and try to speak, you will immediately experience the results. Now imagine the effect when a determined attacker uses both hands with full force. He will have no problem stopping the noise. This is the reason why many victims never get the chance to cry for help. This is where he begins his Power and Control over you!

Once an attacker takes away your ability to call out, you have to understand that he means business. This is for real. He may also hit you, head butt you or smother your mouth with his hand to ensure your silence. The smother usually comes from behind. This is a common military technique used to stop noise as the assailant snaps a neck or pushes a knife into a back. The rapist may well prefer the strangle to the mouth cover-up, to avoid getting bitten.

27

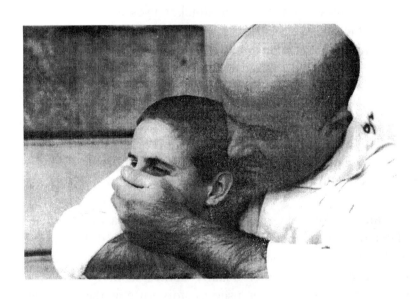

Your neck is your lifeline

- ## The voice-box
  The voice-box (larynx) enables us to speak, to shout and to scream.

- ## The windpipe
  On inhalation oxygen is drawn in through the mouth or the nose and down the windpipe to the lungs, thereby oxygenating the blood. waste gases such as carbon dioxide are expelled on exhalation the same way. this process is known as respiration.

- ## The Carotid Artery
  Oxygenated blood travels to the brain via the carotid artery within the neck.

- ## The Jugular Vein.
  Blood returns to the heart via the jugular vein within the neck.

- ## The Spinal Cord
  The spinal cord runs through the vertebrae of the neck and spinal column. The spinal cord forms part of the central nervous system along which messages are sent to and from the brain.

- ## The Vertebrae
  The 1st & 2nd vertebrae within the neck support the weight of the head and allows it to rotate.

- ## The Carotid Sinus
  Where the Carotid Arteries divide in the upper part of the neck, into the internal and external Carotids, there exists a sensitive pressure receptor called the Carotid Sinus together with adjacent nerves in the sheath of the Artery. These monitor blood pressure as the reflex nerve impulses go from the Carotid Sinus and Sheaf via the Vagal nerve, to the Heart.

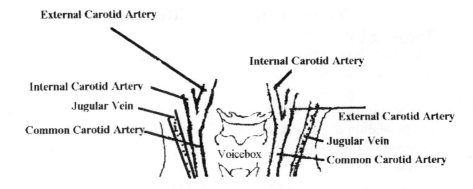

All the above are threatened when our neck is attacked. It is for this reason that we regard our necks as one of our most vulnerable areas. We must learn how to protect this area and to gain release if we are attacked there.

"Mark Ford was jailed for life after he subjected women to violent and perverted attacks weeks after being released from prison for raping a girl of 13.
Mark Ford, was found guilty of two counts of rape and two of kidnap, only six weeks after his release from a seven-year sentence. he snatched a girl of 17. Two weeks later subjected another woman to a rape and torture session in which he burnt her breast with a cigarette lighter. In March 1995 he forced a girl of 16 into his van at knifepoint and raped and abused her."
He used his knowledge of body pressure points to make his victims pass out during their torture

"A man confronted a 28 year old woman after following her, her two-year-old son and six-month-old daughter, along a lane used as a short cut. He held the knife to her pushed her backwards, damaging her neck, and raped her"

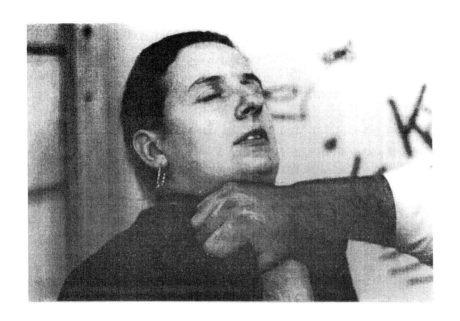

There is no other part of the body, that can be gripped by an attacker, that will so seriously threaten our very existence.

The attacker must not be allowed to gain control of your neck, its your Lifeline !

How long can you hold your breath?

Why should I consider a question like this? The answer is quite simple. Without breath we die. I guess I am not going to get any extra brownie points for answering that one. So, do you know how long you can hold your breath? I conducted an experiment with 2000 females in a secondary school where I teach Self Protection, consisting of groups of twenty, tested over two years. The average time for them was around one minute. Some were able to stretch to one minute thirty seconds, but these had training in swimming under water, knew their limitations and did not panic. Overall these students were fit and healthy and at their pre smoking and alcohol stage of life. What use is this information to you? Well, this would be the time you had to fight off an attacker if he placed an airtight bag over your head.

Consider this attack featured in the **Dagenham Post.** February 1995.

" A 15-YEAR-OLD school boy was subjected to a sickening sex attack after he was attacked by a pervert who put a plastic bag over his head"

In this case the victim was 5 feet 10 inches tall and well built. Fortunately for him there were holes in the bag. The attack lasted for a few minutes. Put yourself in his position. If you were attacked and your nose and mouth were forcibly covered up causing oxygen starvation, the only thing keeping you alive would be the oxygen remaining in your blood. Do you think this would last the full one minute if you were struggling and panicking. **NO!**
Let us halve the time to say 30 or 40 seconds. This is all the time remaining to you as your future is stolen. Well, maybe!

Now for the bad news........ If you are being strangled you may realistically have no more than **6 seconds.**

"In July 1996, 18 year old Nicola Parsons was raped and strangled. Her body was found in a derelict hut asphyxiated with a piece of cloth"

When force is applied to both sides of the neck, the resulting pressure on the right and left carotid arteries (Carotid from a Greek word meaning *" to plunge into deep sleep"*) stops the oxygenated blood from reaching the brain. Only slight pressure is required on the carotid to starve the brain. The result is almost immediate unconsciousness. Compression of the neck also affects the large veins known as the Jugular. These veins return blood from the head to the heart. The pressure inside these veins is low and again, the blood flow can be impeded quite easily.

This leads to the backing up of deoxygenated blood causing congestion and haemorrhaging, whilst the carotid artery, if not shut off through the strangulation, is still pumping more blood into the brain. If you do not get your attacker off your neck immediately you are in big trouble. It will take approximately 10-12 seconds after unconsciousness for irreversible brain death to occur.

Now to bring you even more bad news; A sudden pressure or impact on the Carotid Sinus, which is the sensitive pressure receptor that monitors and controls the blood pressure, can slow down and even stop the reflex nerve impulses to the Heart instantly.

The result is almost instantaneous " **Reflex Cardiac Arrest** " also known as " **Vagal Inhibition** ".

This is a very common cause of death where pressure is applied to the neck, especially in manual strangulation and can occur instantly when the neck is grabbed.

This effect accounts for at least half of the deaths from manual strangulation.

Ever more remarkable causes of sudden death have been recorded due to the Carotid Sinus like drinking a glass of ice cold water, this is how sensitive the Carotid sinus is.

Now return to the previous section entitled **YOUR NECK IS YOUR LIFELINE**. Perhaps you will see things a little more clearly.

Finally, while we are on the subject of the neck, I would like to mention the vertebrae. The 1st vertebrae (atlas) supports the weight of the head, whilst the 2nd vertebrae (axis) allows the head to rotate. A violent, shaking strangulation can damage these vertebrae, causing a whiplash injury.

This could, if serious, be big trouble. If the spinal cord is injured in this area of the neck, the nerves that control breathing could be affected, leading to death from respiratory paralysis.

Now, unless you are junior doctor of the year, much of this information will be new to you. It is essential that you remember it.

"Ruth Hunt, 58 was found dead at her home days after she was strangled, suffocated, and seriously sexually assaulted"

What can you do in a few seconds?

In six seconds you could open your street door, open your car door and get in, dial a telephone number, or put a video tape into your player.

It will take you about six seconds to read two lines of this text. By the time you reach the end of the second line the oxygen supply to your brain could have been cut off.
Unconsciousness will follow. Six seconds is not a long time!

6 Seconds

Am I boring you? I hope not.

I just believe that if you have something important to say, you can not repeat it enough times.

Parents continuously tell their young kids
" This is how you cross the road safely"

"Never get into a stranger's car".

These are examples of messages that can never be repeated too often.

I am telling you that if you are going to be the victim of a rape attack, once the rapist has you by the throat, **you will not have long to escape**.

Armed with your present knowledge of self protection , what would you be able to do?

Here are some options that have been tried by others. **Would any of them work?**

1. You could activate your anti-rape pocket alarm.

2. You could perform a technique learnt from your Martial Arts club.

3. You could scream for help.

4. You could knee your attacker in the Groin.

5. You could play dead and hope he goes away.

6. You could reason with him. Appeal to his sense of decency and fair play.

7. You could tear off your own clothes to get it over and done with.

Be honest . What could you really do in six seconds?

How far are you prepared to go to protect yourself?

If he touches me I will kill him! If you do that again you are dead! If anybody messes with me they know what to expect!

We have all heard such statements time and time again. They are now part of everyday speech.

I want to get into the real world. What are you prepared to do to stay alive?

Would you be able to push a broken glass into an attacker's eyes?
Stick a knife into his neck?
Slash their face with a razor blade?
Bite a finger off?
Break an arm or a leg?

All of these are horrific even to consider. For many decent people they are unthinkable acts. Actually, all of these monstrous assaults were committed against children under 10 years of age or against pensioners. There are scum-bags out there!

Pick any one of the previous assaults and ask yourself if you are capable of doing this in a life threatening situation?
If I said to you that by striking an attacker on the chin, with the bone at the bottom of your palm, you would be able to make him let go, I am sure you would say " no problem".

If, however, I said simply push your finger to the back of his eye socket as deep in as it will go. **Well?**
Or, if your mouth is being covered up by an attacker's hand you could bite a finger. Fine!
But could you bite the finger completely off if that was the only thing that was going to work? Or an ear or nose?

Most civilised people have imposed limits on themselves. They are prepared to go so far, but no further when their own lives are threatened by another. Most of us are far too nice to consider such nastiness. This places us at an enormous disadvantage to the man who is prepared to rape. We need to learn to switch on instant, controlled aggression to survive a rapist's attack and to do whatever is necessary to prevent the attack. Once we have survived, we can become as nice as we want to again.

Strangely enough, we seem to be able to go further when we need to protect others. As children we will take and suffer untold abuse and bullying, but if we see our younger brother or sister on the receiving end we will step in with fists flying.

Many a woman has suffered the physical violence of a partner but if their child becomes the victim, out comes the artillery.

I can remember taking beatings at school and not fighting back. One day I came across a gang of bullies trying to strip my sister. I went berserk, steamed in to the gang and managed to stop the assault. In return I ended up taking a beating myself, but I had managed to stop the assault on my sister. If it had been only been me being bullied, I would have been too scared to stand up for myself.

We must learn to break through this civilised barrier to protect ourselves, as well as others.

The reality is that you could be hurt, abused, raped or tortured if you do not learn to protect yourself. You must do whatever the circumstances require.

If tomorrow, you saw an attacker with his hands around the throat of your child or loved one, you would do whatever was required. The mere thought of facing this type of danger is probably giving you an adrenal rush right now.

You would place no restrictions on what you were prepared to do to save them from harm. I apologise for having to put these very unpleasant thoughts into your head. However, I have to alert you to reality.

If you have not already experienced an assault or worse, at sometime in your life you have unknowingly been at risk or in danger, but your luck has held out.

Faced with the choice of surviving an attack, how far would you go to save yourself?

The fingertip jab to the eyes

The easiest and most effective technique that exists, is the fingertip jab to the eyes.

This is the very first technique that I teach to my students.
It is easy to learn and always works.
If you are able to press a doorbell you already know the technique.
Every time you press a T.V remote control you are training this strike without knowing it and can already perform it, if required in self protection.

How many times have you been temporarily put out of action because a gnat or speck of dust has got into your eye? The items are usually so small that they are difficult to see, yet they can stop you in you tracks. You will be unable to continue until you have removed the object. So, you have experienced the effect a little.

Now try to imagine the effect of getting a finger tip in the eye! Maybe not just a fingertip, maybe the entire finger as it is pushed deep into the socket. However, even in it's most gentle and basic form, a simple touch to the eyes, the attacker's hands will be drawn back from your neck to protect their own eyes.
 " Disgusting!"   *"I could never do that!"* I hear comments like these time and time again.
Let me tell you something.
Whenever I teach my female Self Protection courses, I always begin by teaching the eye jab. I then ask the students to raise their hands if they were prepared to use this technique to defend themselves in a life threatening situation.

The result is usually a 50% split. 50% say that nothing would force them to attack the eyes. After these same students have completed the course, during which I have shown them some of the horrific attacks men are capable of and have generally raised the student's awareness, **all** of them become willing to use the fingertip jab to the eyes. They come to see it as their strongest technique and cannot forget it.

Think back to the earlier section entitled, **WHO ARE WE AFRAID OF?** Remind yourself that violent Man is the one you are afraid of. The reason you fear him is not because he is weaker and less aggressive is it? You fear him because generally, he is bigger, stronger and more aggressive than you are and he intends taking power and control of your body! So, if you can not match these attributes *you must find a weak link*. The weak link is those eyeballs. No matter how many weights our macho-man lifts, no matter how much punching they practice on the bags or press-ups they do, they can do nothing about this natural weakness. Their eyes can not be strengthened, so use this weakness to your advantage.

Another thing to consider is that we have been talking about a lone fingertip jab to the eyes. What about the other fingers and thumbs of both hands? Throw the lot in and you will see how your chance of success has multiplied greatly. If you have long fingernails as well, your weaponry becomes devastating.

As an experiment, ask a friend to hold two large soft tomatoes at head height as a target for you to aim at. Using both hands, push your fingertips in and out of the targets as many times as you can manage within six seconds. After the time is up, count the number of individual finger strikes that you were able to perform.

If you only performed one strike a second with your eight fingers that would be forty eight individual strikes to the eyes. Bearing in mind that one tiny fly can put an eye out of action, what would forty eight fingertip jabs do?

"Stephen Laudat stabbed Bryan Bennett 82 times in a 15-minute attack that only ended when police arrived and disarmed him"

41

If I were to be put in the position in which I was only able to teach one technique, a technique that would serve someone throughout their life, it would be the fingertip jab.

There is not a person on this earth who could withstand the fingertip jab to the eyes.

Skill and technique versus strength

Whenever a student joins a class of mine for the first time, they almost always regard their strength, or lack of it as their only weapon. The truth is that strength is far less important in self protection than most believe it to be. It is not the way to win. You cannot beat strength with strength unless of course you are always stronger than your opponent. Even then victory is not always assured.

Big fish eat little fish, yet little fish survive by using skill and technique.

How would David have got on if he had tried to use his strength against Goliath?

Good Doormen or "Bouncers", have to use the skilful application of the law, communication skills, body language and acting to avoid fighting all the time. Those who do fight all the time are mostly doing so through choice.

Talking your way out of a fight or possible sexual assault is using a form of skill and technique. If this is unsuccessful or this option is taken away because you have been ambushed you can fall back on another skill, such as the finger jab to the eyes. We already know that this technique, if used swiftly, will match any show of strength. Now try this little experiment:-

Find a friend and face each other. Ask them to place their right hand flat on your left shoulder. Let them push you backwards gently, but progressively. Now you begin to resist their pushing by pushing your left shoulder forward. This is purely strength matching strength and of course, the strongest of you will win. Now, do the same thing but after resisting for a few seconds, push you friend's right arm at the wrist, to your left with your right hand whilst turning your shoulders in anti clockwise direction.

This is skill and technique versus strength. Which of the two methods makes more sense?

Remember what I said just now about body language, mannerisms etc.?

Please do not think that I am only referring here to physical techniques.

Have you heard the expression "The pen is mightier then the sword"? This refers to one method of controlling and overcoming brute force without needing to use physical strength namely, the Law, the courts, intelligent debate etc. Of course we need force to back up our legal system but only in a minority of cases.

Bruce Lee, the martial artist, was a great believer in the art of **"Fighting without Fighting"**. Watch the film **Enter the Dragon** for an example of tricking an opponent into defeat before a fight can start. Psyching out an aggressor is another effective method, if you are a good actor!

Probably your best weapon is **common-sense**. If you are in a night-club and find a guy getting heavy with you, tell him that you need to use the loo, but instead ask a doorman to see you safely to your car or a cab. If you find yourself being followed whilst driving, divert to a police station, fire station etc. rather than stopping and risking a physical assault. I will talk about a number of such skills and techniques as we progress.

Finally, never be misled into thinking such methods of avoiding violent encounters are for cowards only. Backing off and backing down are two different things. There are too many dead heroes!

You may have to fight for your life, in which case it will help if you can fight, but it is better to be able to get out of the situation without violence ever starting.

If he slaps you he doesn't love you!

Domestic violence is ugly and illegal but, sadly, it happens and will continue to happen. For whatever reason many women put up with abuse and beatings from their partner and will never do anything to help themselves. Consider this true life case study of a victim of domestic violence.

"He started beating me, he had hit me before but this time the beatings continued. I didn't put up a fight, I knew he was too strong for me. It did not stop there. He poured boiling water over my face, shoulders and arms, then into my mouth. It scalded my lungs. He also fractured my skull and jaw. My mum found me unconscious on the bed the next day. She didn't recognise me. I was taken to hospital. I had drips in my feet and hand and a tube in my mouth. I was close to death. It was three months before I came round. I was still wearing an oxygen mask then. I am now in a wheelchair and relearning to walk, my hair is slowly growing back and my head and neck is covered in scars. My two year old son looks at older photographs of me prior to the attack and says that is his other mummy."

This is a real life horror story that tells of the extremes of domestic violence. In this case it lead to a charge of attempted murder. Most cases are not so life threatening but, in my opinion, are no less serious. My advice is to get out of any relationship that subjects you to any form of abuse as soon as the first exposure to common assault has taken place i.e. as soon as you have been put into fear for your safety and before you have been physically assaulted.

Domestic violence is a crime and you should remember that nobody has the right to assault you either physically, sexually or emotionally. Everyone is entitled to live their life free from the fear of abuse and violence. As a victim you may feel isolated, humiliated, ashamed and confused but, you need not suffer in silence. Help is available. Remember that it is the person committing the assault, that has the problem, but you need to act to make them accept the responsibility for this violence. They need to change their behaviour.

Domestic violence knows no boundaries and comes in many guises. It can be a physical assault, sexual abuse, rape, threats, mental or verbal abuse, humiliation, money deprivation, constant criticism, being denied access to your friends or relatives and so on, Its the old male bullshit power and control thing again.

Indefinitely. These acts will fall into one of the three categories of *simple, serious or life threatening.*

In all cases of domestic violence you should never come to believe that you will only get one chance to seek help. You can ask for help whenever you need it, until you gain the strength to go all the way and end the relationship. You must never play down the abuse you suffer and you should realise that there is no excuse whatsoever that justifies being abused by a person who, supposedly cares for you.

You can contact the following numbers for help:-

Women's Aid England 0117 963 3542
Welsh Women's Aid 01222 390874

Both of these agencies will give you more local numbers that you can call. Most local groups run 24 hours a day and their services are completely free and more importantly, **confidential.**

Many women stay in abusive relationships because they fear the financial implications of breaking free. General advice about Social Security benefits for you and any children who may be involved, is available by calling Freeline **Social Security on 0800 666 555**.

Housing is also a serious consideration, but help will be available through your local housing office. If you have to leave your home due to violence you **will not** be seen as deliberately making yourself homeless, so the council may have a legal obligation to help you.

The Council will be able to provide temporary accommodation at once, until a suitable long term place is available.

If you have children, you should seek advice from your local Women's Aid Group, Law Centre, Citizen's Advice Bureau or a solicitor regarding **contact orders, residential orders, parental responsibilities**, change of school and all those related matters to do with the safety and welfare of your children .

In my time as an advice worker for the Citizen's Advice Bureau, I came to realise that the main thing that stopped people from taking action and gaining control of their own affairs, was the fact that they were not aware of the help and advice that was available, to allow them to gain the confidence to take the first steps to escape. Never hesitate. Get in contact with the people who can offer help.

You may be at the stage, where you really want to call the police, but you have always avoided this because you have been led to believe that the police can't do anything and are not interested anyway. You may be under the illusion that the police will tell you that the problem is not for the them to settle as it is a private matter between you and your partner. **WRONG! WRONG! WRONG!**

The police have specially trained male and female officers experienced in dealing with domestic violence victims. They will treat you sympathetically and talk to you away from your partner. They will be able to arrange for you to receive medical aid if necessary and locate a safe place for you to go.

To contact the police in an emergency dial 999 or you can contact your local police station and ask to speak to the domestic violence unit. Your enquiry will be completely confidential and they will offer you the help you'll need.

Sadly, I know that many women will continue to suffer abuse **'for the sake of the children'** or in the hope that 'things will change' or a multitude of other reasons. They would probably take none of the advice I have given. So, I am going to offer some further advice, advice that really goes against the grain.

To accept this advice means **that you have decided to remain in the abusive relationship** and as I have said, this is a mistake.

I watched my mother make the same mistake when I was still a child. This mistake led her into as much humiliation, insult and physical and mental pain as any woman has suffered in an abusive relationship. It resulted in two suicide attempts and admittance to a mental hospital before the real problem was addressed i.e. the abusive relationship.

My mother could not find the courage to leave. It was only when the physical abuse became directed at her children that she decided to act and face the aggressor head on. Following this confrontation, domestic violence in our family came to an end. But all this left unanswered questions in my mind. Why did two children almost lose a mother twice through attempted suicide? Why did we have to see our mother so mentally abused that she entered a mental hospital and, for some time, failed to recognise her own children when we visited her?

The abuse started with 'mere' threats. Soon these threats led to actual physical violence. My mother's head was split open on a fireplace, she was hit with a glass ash tray, her body was used to stub out live cigarettes and so on. All this was all on one occasion only. I have personally witnessed many forms of domestic violence as a child so I can appreciate the difficulty you face leaving the situation but leaving is the only real solution.

However, if you do decide to stay and to try to weather the storm, here reluctantly, is my advice for your own self protection.

As a female the odds are that most men you will come across will be stronger than you. This is not being sexist. **I live in the real world and accept the laws of reality which do not take into account political correctness**.

Let's look at an imaginary situation.

In the family home the mother and father are having a row.

When the father decides it's time to win and show that he means business he immediately tenses up, becomes aggressive and he strikes the table with his fists in a display of strength. Pathetic isn't it? It happens all the time. Its that Power and control that he wants.

Now, if she tries to match this display and starts to bang her fists in the same manner, all this will do is to make him even more aggressive. He will feel that his 'superiority' is being challenged, his power and control is being threatened, he will not be able to back down and will have to prove himself with an even more aggressive display. Can you see how we are steadily moving towards violence?

This is the moment to stop things escalating.

This is where women should use their intelligence. Now is the time to become passive, to back down in a no win situation. Do not take him to the point of no return, let the man think that he has won. Don't challenge his power and control. Now he doesn't have to resort to violence. He has not really won anything, Your opinions haven't changed at all **but you haven't been hit**. You have let him have his power and control at a level that stops the violence.

Now, I can hear you saying **"that's bullshit! I can't back down."** But remember it's you who wants to stay in this hopeless and dangerous situation. I have already advised you to get out. If you do choose to stay, the only answer is to pacify your aggressive partner to avoid the inevitable blows. You should not have to put up with this type of crap from men.

**You must learn to do whatever is necessary to protect yourself.**

Here are some pointers to surviving in this situation if you chose to remain with a violent partner:-

1. Learn how to calm down an aggressive situation.
2. Learn to act in a passive manner to diffuse your partner's anger.
3. Learn how to keep your own aggression in control.
4. Do not issue challenges that threaten his desired power and control.
5. Learn how to switch off your partner's aggression without letting him know that it is you who is in control of the situation.
6. Learn the art of deception to trick your partner into reading submission when actually you have not submitted at all.

Are you getting the idea? Deception has always been a great weapon in warfare.

If all of these techniques of evasion fail during one particular domestic dispute and violence is about to occur and you cannot escape, you will have to fight back.
The risk here is that unless you are immediately successful, your partner's aggression may be increased still further. If you are going to use a physical strike you must use it exactly as you would if it were a stranger attacking you.
This situation is no different!

You must be able to stop your attacker otherwise you will get hurt. Please remember your body is your body. No one has the right to hurt, abuse, or take power and control of you. If you can recognise even the mildest form of abuse in any of your current relationship, get out now.

Don't wait until it is too late. Stop hoping and kidding yourself that things may get better. Prevention is the best cure. Put this book down and phone one of the numbers I have given to you. That one call will probably turn your life around completely and you will get back in control of your life.

APPLY SELF PROTECTION NOW AND SO AVOID SELF DEFENCE LATER.

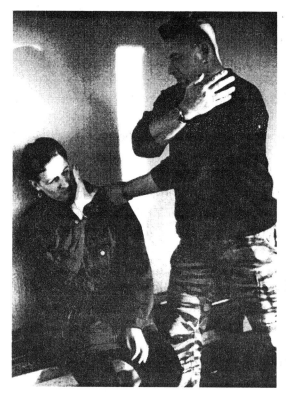

"SARA Thornton was jailed for life for the murder of her violent husband after suffering years of abuse. She stabbed him to death with a kitchen knife in 1989. She later went on hunger strike in prison in 1991 after hearing that a man who killed his alcoholic wife had received a two-year suspended sentence when <u>the court accepted his plea of provocation.</u>"

"Emma Humphreys who spent more than 10 years in prison after being convicted in 1985 of stabbing and murdering her violent boyfriend, who regularly terrorised, beat and raped her during the time they lived together, has now been freed by the Court of Appeal."

The groin secret that is no secret

OK! Ladies, the alarm clock has just gone off. It is time to wake up!

For generations our parents have kindly passed on a well kept secret that runs something like this:

IF A MAN TRIES IT ON WITH YOU OR ATTACKS YOU, JUST KICK HIM IN THE BALLS.

Get a life!
Do you really think that this so called secret has slipped by the entire male population?
Do you think that men are totally unaware of the danger? I don't think so.

Just as a woman understands that the first time she has full intercourse, she loses her virginity, so a man knows that a kick in the groin will cause him serious pain.

As men, we have to carry our testicles around with us each and every day. We get it down to a fine art protecting them from accidents and intentional strikes. Can't you see that most attackers understand full well that you are going to try to attack this vulnerable area.

They know your little secret. Father Christmas is a better kept secret!

Imagine the attacker who is intent on raping you. He is fully aware that he needs his genital area to work if he is to succeed. He also appreciates fully the vulnerability of the area.. He knows for sure that a strike in the groin will cripple him.

He will not give you that chance.

If you were to get into a ring with a boxer, he would not be surprised if you tried to punch him.
If you were alone with a rapist, he would not be surprised if you tried to attack his groin.

However, don't get me wrong. If you were to get the chance, go for it, but do not rely on it or con yourself into thinking you have some secret defence technique up your sleeve.

Consider this:
How often do you hear or read in the news of a rapist being defeated by a mere kick in the groin?

Ans: Never

The state of women's self defence

Traditionally women's self defence has been taught in evening classes alongside other subjects such as Oriental Tea making and Underwater Basket Weaving. The classes are usually attended by bored females with time to kill. In these classes they will learn a few Martial art techniques from the particular style the martial arts instructor specialises in and after a few weeks, are packed off believing that they know how to protect themselves.

Whenever these techniques fail in practice **and most of them will**, women lose confidence in their ability and lose heart in further learning. The problem is that these women have been misled. They have been sold misinformation.

If I advised a young girl who required sex education advice, that the safest form of contraception was to practice the rhythm and withdrawal method , I would rightly be considered ignorant of the facts. If, as a result of this advice the girl later fell pregnant I, the adviser would share some of the responsibility.

This is exactly what is happening in women's self protection. **Misinformation, useless techniques and no foundation**. No wonder most women give up or just carry on attending the classes for the social life.

I believe one of the fundamental failings of most self defence courses for women is that they lack any real theoretical base. If all that you are taught is to practice a few movements without any appreciation of why you are doing them, you are wasting your time. **THEORY IS ESSENTIAL.**

Even the word **'defence'** relates to an attack *that has already happened*. I prefer to use the term **'protection,'** which focuses on awareness, evaluation and avoidance and bears no relation to waiting for an attack to happen.

I actually believe that the future, for female self protection, will consist of the greater percentage being theory and the lesser part containing the physical practice.

What, for instance, would you consider to be of more value for the a female?

1. A programme of instruction aimed at producing female Rambos.
2. A programme that teaches awareness, evaluation and avoidance of dangerous situations.

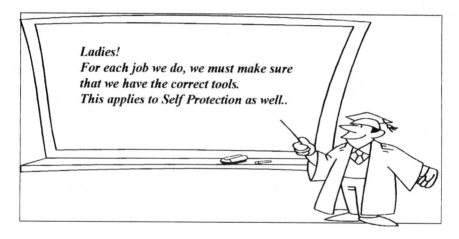

I am not trying to say here that all physical techniques are worthless. There are some that are well suited to women and do work. However, most are greatly overrated and the wrong tools considering the type of threat that exists.

The moment that women's self protection escapes the clutches of traditional martial arts and the word **'defence' is replaced by 'protection'**, is the moment learning will begin and a new respect will be born.

Beware stereotypes!

Take a look at any stranger and tell me whether you think that they are a smoker, a vegetarian, gay, a car owner, a racist, a good lover, a computer user or so on. Probably you will get it wrong!

Take me , for instance, people take one look at me and make an instant judgement.

He <u>must</u> be a smoking, gambling, kebab eating, football hooligan.

Actually, I have never smoked, have never been in a betting shop, I hate football and I'm a vegetarian.

Yet, being the world's first failed anorexic carrying excess relaxed muscle (fat), having a bashed up face, and a football crazy son, nobody finds out what I'm really like unless they spend time getting to know me.

Stereotyping me is no great problem unless you are trying to force a dead cow and 100 cigarettes down my throat. I am just trying to show you how it is our usual practice to make an instant judgement, based on stereotypes, which could easily be wrong.

We associate a raincoat or plastic Mac with the dirty old man or flasher. A gay man must be limp wristed with a high, feminine voice and lesbians must be muscular, butch, tattooed characters with deep voices.

We are making a big mistake by relying on such simplistic stereotypes.

If you create such a picture in your mind of the rapist or mugger, you will get tunnel vision. You will miss the clean cut, respectable looking guy who could rape you on a train or when he gives you a lift home one evening.

The only feature common to all male attackers is their penis and their intent to use it, if it is a sexual attack. Do not be deceived.

Do not focus all your attention on the lager lout who may be totally harmless, and miss the business man next to him who may be the true threat.

Remember the story of The Trojan Horse?
The attacking Greek soldiers deceived the defending Trojans by hiding inside a huge wooden horse. The Trojans pulled the horse inside their city. During the night the Greeks climbed down from the horse, killed the guards and let their own army in through the gates. The city of Troy fell.

Moral? **Always expect the unexpected! Try to see beneath the surface appearance, things are not always as they seem.**

" In November 95, an 81 year old woman was raped at knifepoint by a man who tricked his way into her home apparently claiming to be from the BBC television programme Crimewatch UK "

What stereotype assessment will you make of the above group ?
I bet it's not canary breeders, stamp collectors, or vicars.
The truth is, they all teach and promote Female self protection.

Where men can pose a threat to you

In certain places and at certain times, a man will not be a threat to you. However, change the place or the time and that same man will be a threat. Here are some examples to start you thinking:

Example 1.
You are at home with your parents when a door to door salesman calls. Your parents are interested in the product on offer. They invite the salesman in. The salesman notices you and during the course of the conversation, asks which school you attend. The salesman leaves and the conversation is forgotten. In this situation the guy has not posed a direct threat. However, a few days later, as you are on your way home from school, a car pulls up at the bus stop where you are waiting. It is the salesman. It is raining, the bus is overdue and you are late home, the salesman kindly offers you a lift. He says he is on his way to your home anyway, to finish his business with your parents, he is taking control. The threat begins!

Example 2.
You are in a night-club with a group of your friends. You are in a safe environment. There is no immediate risk. However, there is a man scanning the club for any girls who are a bit tipsy. He follows you home on foot or by car. He approaches you as soon as you have left your friends. The threat begins!

Example 3.
Some guy who you know well stops you whilst you are out shopping. He seems a bit agitated. He says you must return home immediately. There has been an accident at home, your mother has hurt herself in a fall. He will give you a lift. Of course you are worried, panic starts to set in, the adrenaline starts to flow. You run to the car with him and jump in. Deprived of time stolen by worry, there is no time for logical thinking. He has control.
The threat begins!

Example 4.
You are in the office at the end of the day. Your male Boss asks you to stay an extra half hour to finish some important work. You agree. The safe office environment of the daytime is no longer so safe. The two of you are alone together. The threat begins!

This one is for real.

"Gillian Montgomery, 53, was beaten very violently and stabbed to death with a single stab wound to her neck in her flat by a man pretending to work for a water company."

They all have one thing in common however. The threat begins when you find yourself **alone with a man with no witnesses. In these circumstances you are much more likely to face an attack.**

To avoid threatening situations, try to stay within eye contact of another person other than the man who could pose the threat. It is a good idea to scan your week and to note all those times when you could find yourself in a threatening situation.

When might you be alone with a man?

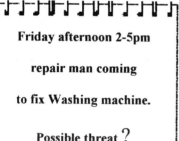

Friday afternoon 2-5pm

repair man coming

to fix Washing machine.

Possible threat ?

Once you have made a note of such situations try to think of ways to avoid the possible threat. Remember that attacks happen in crowded places too, but these are much more rare.

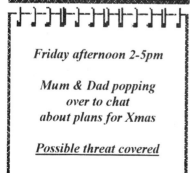

Friday afternoon 2-5pm

Mum & Dad popping over to chat about plans for Xmas

Possible threat covered

I HOPE THIS RAISES YOUR AWARENESS AND ALERTS YOU TO POSSIBLE THREATS.

The calculated attacker

The classic situation occurs when you find yourself at a party and a man encourages you to drink more and more. Of course you do not want to be classed as a killjoy or prude in front of your mates, so you drink more than you really want. Your defence's start to come down. This often happens to young girls who want to be one of the crowd.

You must realise that the man is after one thing only. SEX.

The alcohol is a means to an end for him. If you get drunk, a sexual attack could come without you knowing a thing about it.
Men are well aware that if you drink too much you will need help to get home. You will not be able to drive your car, maybe not even able to walk without help.
This places you at their mercy if you are alone with them, at the end of the evening.
They begin to gain their power and control.
I have known men to turn away cabs that women have ordered after having one drink too many and then gallantly offering them a lift home to try their luck.
I have known men getting a mate to pretend to be a cab driver and then, as planned, the car breaks down on the way home.
I know of one guy who deflated a girl's car Tyre before she left the pub and then offered her a lift home.
When you start to drink in pubs and clubs, even at home alone with your boyfriend, **beware of the spiked drinks**. It happens. **Drugs have been known to have been dropped into food and drinks undetected.**
I know, it has happened to me.

"John Blackman was found guilty of three charges of indecent assault and committing a sex act in 1994. He administered an overpowering drug to the woman, injected her whilst she was in a comatose state, shaved off her pubic hair, then carried out a sex act"

Here is an unpleasant example from my own experience.
This is for real!

A young lad got a female friend so drunk she passed out completely, he had full power and control. The boy then stripped her clothes off and proceeded to take photographs of her in indecent poses, with an instant developing film. The boy then dressed her again. She awoke a few hours later completely unaware of the incident.

A few days later she met the boy again. He told her that before she became unconscious, she had asked him for sex and begged him to take photographs of her. He told her that she would have to agree to regular sex with him in order to get the photographs back (Power and control).

The distressed girl confided with one of her friends, who I happened to be teaching. I was told of the incident and was asked to help. I paid a visit to the boy's home and encouraged him to hand over the photographs and also, tape record a true version of his abuse of this girl. I left with the photos and tape, gave them to the girl and advised her to inform the police. End of story.

Some men will use alcohol or drugs as weapons to make their attempt of power and control easier. Watch out for this.

I read this from a local newspaper while in America.

" Four men were recently successfully prosecuted for rape in Florida after knocking their victims out with Rohypnol, a sleeping pill sold in chemist's shops throughout Europe. The pills, commonly known as roofies, are being slipped into the victims drinks " June 96

They are sold on city streets for around less than £1 each.

Frightening isn't it.

STAY ALERT AND SWITCHED ON

NEVER UNDERESTIMATE THE LENGTHS SOME MEN WILL GO TO GET WHAT THEY WANT.

The dangers of travelling to and from school

To beat the aggressor at his own game we need to begin to see things from his point of view. Get inside his head.

Let us look at the risks posed by journeys to and from school. I talk here of girls but, of course, the same applies to young boys.

Which do you think poses the greatest threat, the journey to school or the journey home?

This is a question I ask of all the girls I teach.
The most common answer is, **coming home from school is the most dangerous**. **WRONG!** I will explain why.

Thinking as an abductor, I know that from the moment you are missed the panic buttons will be pushed by your parents. If your parents or guardian are expecting you home for 4.30 p.m. and school finishes at 4 p.m., they will begin to worry when you are 10 minutes overdue. After 20-30 minutes, they will be on the phone to the school or to your friends in search of you. Within an hour they will be phoning the police if there is still no sign of you. By the time the police visit your home and start making enquiries as little as two hours may have passed.

Now, what about the alternative of abducting you on your way to school?
The man now has from 9 a.m. until the time you usually arrive home say 4.15 p.m., to make his escape. **SEVEN HOURS.**
Even if your school has a policy of phoning your parents or guardian when your name is not answered on the register, this may not be done until late morning. Your parents may not be there to take the call.
Even if they do take the call, they may think that you have skipped a lesson and may not become concerned immediately.

If your parents work, they may not arrive home until much later than you. This could give your abductor up to **12 hours** before the alarm bells ring.
Bad News.

There are other advantages to snatching a victim as they travel to school, which may not be immediately obvious to the average law abiding citizen.

He knows that to snatch a school girl **he need only look out for a recognisable school uniform**. From this he will know which school you are attending, which route you are most likely taking to school and when you are due to arrive. From these basics he will be able to work out the best place to approach you.

Unlike the time you leave school with all your mates, most kids travel to school on their own. Less witnesses! Furthermore, if the abductor were to take you after school he would need to make his escape during the rush hour, before school the rush hour is coming to an end.

This is chilling, unpleasant stuff, I agree, but by looking at things the way an attacker does, light can be thrown on ways to beat him.

Once again do not trap yourself by dropping your guard.

You must also consider the risk during your lunch break, or if you need to leave school to travel to a sports field or centre.

Work out a foolproof system that will ensure your safety.

Release and escape

The ability to release yourself from an attacker's initial hold is very important You must be able to break the link instantly, thereby avoiding further complications. You must destroy his power and control over you but watch out for his ego.

I have mentioned the stranglehold, but there are many more including headlocks, arm-locks, clothing holds and even handshake holds. Infact any part of your body or clothing which can be held or grabbed like a handle, will allow a hold. The initial hold is designed to restrain you temporarily, but will almost certainly be followed by more permanent measures, if you delay your escape.

Such measures may involve cuffs, string, rope, scarves, plastic cable ties and so on.

All such methods are designed to rob you of the means of escaping and to neutralise any skill or technique you may have. Further forms of entrapment can then be put into effect by your attacker such as the following example taken from THE TIMES July 1995,

RAPIST CONVICTED.
"Brett Mills, who bound a girl, aged 12, bundled her in a suitcase and took her by taxi to a friend's flat where he abused and raped her, was found guilty of rape, wounding and false imprisonment by the Old Bailey".

Mail sacks, boxes, car boots and, as in the above example, a suitcase , have all been used to hold victims against their wills.

"In may 1996 John Blackman was found guilty, and jailed for 9 years, on 6 charges of rape, one of attempted rape, false imprisonment and indecent assault at Maidstone Crown court after holding a teenage girl captive for three days as his sex slave in his flat in Deptford"

Still more callous methods may include breaking bones in the hands, feet, ankles etc. to stop a victim escaping.

You will now understand from the above examples, why breaking the initial hold is so vital. It is of paramount importance that you stop the attacker from incapacitating you after the early attack.

The best way is to react instantly, without thought and with full commitment applying every ounce of theoretical and physical knowledge that you can apply from this book and other common-sense resources.

You must break free from his hold and deny him having power and control over you....

"A DRIVER who knocked over a woman put her in the boot of his car and drove off because he thought she was dead, Donna Hayes, 33, said she was released when the motorist heard her banging on the inside of the boot after she regained consciousness.

"I remember knocking on the boot - but I cannot recall how many times I had to do it before the car stopped. I don't know how long I was in the boot but when I got out I was a couple of miles from where I had been walking. he said he thought I was dead and had put me in the boot,"

The law and the pre-emptive strike

What is the Pre-emptive Strike? Why do you need to know how the Law relates to the Pre-emptive Strike?

A Pre-emptive strike is a strike against an attacker, made by his victim, before the attacker strikes the victim. The alternative is for the victim to wait until they have been physically assaulted before striking back (if they are able to).

So when could you perform a Pre-emptive strike?

'The Law states that if the antagonist (attacker) is aggressive and moving forward, and you fear for your safety, you can legally, Pre-emptively strike the first blow in *SELF DEFENCE'*.

You could perform such a strike when you were **placed in fear for your safety** by an assailant's action. Even though you may not have been physically touched, you are entitled in Law to use *reasonable* force in self-defence, to protect yourself. This reasonable force is most likely to take the form of a physical strike.

You will be performing this strike, before the attacker strikes you, because *the circumstances of the attack have led you to fear for your safety.* You know an attack is about to happen and you are striking, in self-defence, in order to survive the attack and not endure actual physical harm to yourself.

This is the Pre-emptive Strike.

If you would like to find out more about this area of the Law, try to get hold of the latest edition of 'Butterworth's Police Law' from your library. This is the criminal law book used by the police themselves.

The underlined sentence above is very important for you to understand. I would advise you to memorise it.

If an attack does take place involving you and it is your attacker who gets seriously injured rather than you, **what you say after the event, is vital for your own case. Even though you were acting purely in self defence**, you must remember that you were **in fear for your own safety.**

As you were genuinely in fear for your own safety the attacker has committed a crime, namely Common Assault. This breach of the Law entitles you to launch you Pre-emptive strike in self defence.

Here is a simple analogy,
A wasp flies near you. Naturally, you fear you are about to be stung. In effect, the wasp has committed a Common Assault. Without thinking any more about it you launch your Pre-emptive strike. You are acting in self defence.

You do not wait to be stung first before swatting the wasp.

I have not really taught you anything new here, have I ? Hopefully, I have just increased your awareness that what applies to wasps also applies to rapists and other attackers. You do not have to wait until you are physically attacked, you do not have to hand over the power and control of your body to legally strike your assailant. However, **you must try to stay within the Law.**

The Pre-emptive strike is there to be used and not abused!
If you do *not* genuinely fear for your safety, you are not in a legal position to strike first.

Your defence must be reasonable

I consider myself to be a lover of life and try hard to show respect to those people around me. I am generally a passive, laid back introvert. I prefer to avoid physical confrontations whenever I can, hoping to settle problems through discussion. Sadly, some people take my discussion approach as a sign of weakness and proceed to try physical application to get their point across.

This attitude really pisses me off! I hate it when someone forces me along the path of violence. They force my preference to change.
If the situation does deteriorate into violence, I always try to remind myself of the possible consequences.
We could both be taking a trip in a police van, ambulance or hearse, all because some arsehole mistook me for an easy target.

So, what do I do?
This bloke is seriously pushing his luck. I am sure I can deal with the situation (otherwise I would be attempting to run the four minute mile by now!) I am a pissed off with a fighting ability capable of taking a life, without using weapons, very quickly.
If he grabs me I could break his grip, destroy his attack and then proceed to discipline him like he would never forget.
I know what I am capable of. He would end up pulverised and I would become the ' have a go ' hero. Right?   **No! Wrong!**
The reality is, I could find myself with a **Grievous Bodily Harm** case against me and a free ride in a police car to the station. Where did I go wrong?   *I was only defending myself, officer!*

Well! the Law states *that*

'It is both good Law and good sense that a person who is attacked may defend themselves but that in doing so, they may only do what is reasonably necessary'.
You can rightfully defend yourself but *nothing more*.

No returning the attack with added interest. No breaking your attacker's arms and legs and biting his nose off because he threatened to slap your face.
The Law is quite clear on the matter.

You may only respond with a self defence technique, that right minded people would accept as reasonable, according to the type of attack.

If you were to grab me with the obvious intention of harming me and I retaliated by punching you on the chin, most people would accept that I had acted reasonably. However, if I proceeded to stamp on your head when you fell to the floor, I would be using excessive and unnecessary force.

Here is the deal.

I see a person moving towards me making threatening remarks and gestures.
I assess the situation and evaluate my options. If I cannot avoid the confrontation and I am in fear for my safety. I can launch my Pre-emptive strike. However, this is the real world and it is easy to miss the moment.

Maybe I was not switched on when the guy first made his move, so I lost the chance of making a Pre-emptive strike. Shit happens!!

I must still remember to remain inside the Law. I can only do what is reasonable to stop the attack. If I knock the man to the floor I may have a new option, namely escaping.

If I proceed to jump up and down on him for five minutes I would have overstepped the mark.

The Law can work on a fine line and you must be aware of your responsibilities as well as your rights.

Is it, Simple, serious or life threatening

The name of the game here is **evaluation**. Check out the situation and make an assessment of the level of risk you are faced with. This may not be as easy as it sounds.

Here is an example:

You are walking down the road when you feel a kick to your backside. This kick hurt you and made the adrenaline flow. You have been placed in a position of *fearing for your safety* and your assailant has undoubtedly committed a common assault. You are entitled to defend yourself.

You have practised the Pre-emptive strike that suits you best and you have got the green light to go, or have you? Life is full of surprises. Remember what I wrote a little while back? **Always expect the unexpected!!**
You are turning round, ready to let fly with your fingertip jab to the eyes, when you discover that your attacker is an eight year old boy. He has been dared by his pals to kick you to prove his 'bottle'. So, do you let fly with your lethal strike?

Or, upon turning around, your attacker turns out to be a friend of yours jokingly testing out your reaction, after hearing that you have been attending self protection classes.

Or, it is an old boy who has just been thrown out of a pub and has kicked out at the pub door in anger, missed and caught you instead. Do you go for the eyes with your finger jab?

Or, it turns out to be a nutter who wants to take power and control of your body to rape you.

Do you use the Pre-emptive strike now?

The solution to the problem lies in evaluating the situation as it occurs.

You must decide if the situation is

a] Simple,   **b] Serious**   **c] Life Threatening**.

Once you have made this decision, you must then decide the degree of self protection that is acceptable in Law to both sufficiently be of use to you yet remain lawful.

So, how exactly do you make this essential evaluation?

What follows is my own method which I apply to the value I put on my own life.

a] The Simple Threat.

At this level a **Non Physical** common assault may have taken place. It may be prior to or at the point of fearing for your safety. However, you judge the situation and feel that no real physical threat appears to be intended and that it can be successfully resolved without responding with violence. Some of the examples given above are of this kind. However, if the situation goes the other way and becomes uglier, we are moving towards the next stage.

b] The Serious Threat.

A situation may begin at this level or may have evolved from a simple threat being mishandled or not having its desired effect.
We need to try and reduce the stage of risk **back to a simple threat**, If the situation is not taking a backward step and is clearly moving forward **you have a serious threat on your hands**.

You now feel that the encounter is going to become harmful to you. The possibility of you becoming hurt, cut, broken boned, and feeling pain now is what on offer on today's menu.

The attacker has decided and made it clear that they are going to take power and control of this next moment of your life and is prepared to cause you suffering in the process.

At this stage when you feel that reasoning and all other non physical responses are out of the question. You must realise that your assailant means you serious harm. He intends to inflict pain on you and visions of a hospital bed appear within your realms. In Law the effect of his actions will be called **Grievous Bodily Harm.**

You have assessed and decided that there is no other alternative other than to strike first. So, you will have to launch a Pre-emptive strike in order to stop the attacker.

If you miss the opportunity as happens in the real world, or your response to the situation is a little out of time , you must fight back with all the violence that the attacker forces you to use, in order to stop the attack and minimise your physical suffering as far as possible.

c] The Life Threatening Attack.
This is the big one, when life as you know it is threatened. Your attacker may also be armed with a weapon. He may tell you he intends to use the weapon or make's serious life threats against you. You are left in no doubt, either by his words or his action's, that your life is at risk.
I personally consider rape, or loss of my eyesight or mobility as life threatening to me because any of these will drastically alter the quality of **my own personal life** for the worse and force a major change on any future that I have left.

I class life threatening as something that is going to take away your life as you live it now.
What if your right to live that life, as you do now, is going to be taken away from you?

Its just like being put in prison for the remainder of your life and being forced to live in a different way.

For me life threatening is much wider than the obvious biological definition of living or dying.

Life threatening to me includes my **" quality of life"** as I live it now and how this encounter is going to change that. Your values that you apply to your own life may differ to mine.

In a life threatening situation my advice is, to *do anything in your power to survive*. You should draw from your resources anything you can to keep you alive or keep your life as it is now.. Of course nothing in life is clear cut , but I believe these three levels of threat evaluation make good sense and, if you understand them, will act as reliable guides.

The knockout

The most effective method of knocking someone out has, somehow, been lost in the fighting arts and needs to be reintroduced to any form of self protection that claims to be informed and effective.
The basics of this forgotten method are quite simple.

Strike the tip of your attacker's chin with any solid bone in your own body that has the capability of swift movement and your attacker will go down.

Impose restrictions upon yourself like only hitting softly or without commitment and you begin to lose the ability. The range of movement your chosen bone weapon has, is important here.
It would not be realistic to try to use your hip or a rib as an effective weapon for obvious reasons. However, the human body does contain a surprisingly large number of very useful weapons in this category.
I will list a few of them below.

1) **The closed fist**
As used in a boxing style jab (lead hand) or cross (same punch but with rear hand). These strikes allow the **bony** knuckles of the closed fists to strike the chin **bone**.
Personally, I favour the jab because if it's devastating speed and power. A skilled puncher could jab in a mere one tenth of a second, a blink of the eye.
The cross takes a fraction longer to execute, but is usually more powerful. When either of these strikes connect properly, it very unlikely that your assailant will remain standing.
Generally, I do not teach punching on my female Self Protection classes because it takes a long time to get a quality punch together, however with more females taking up a mixture of Boxing and Aerobic training, it is only right that I include the fist in this book.

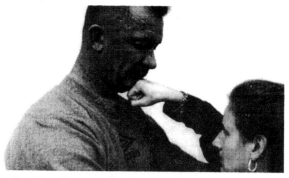

2) **The Palm-heel strike**.

This strike is excellent if you are really in close to your attacker, even close enough as to feel your attacker's breath on your face. In this situation just drive your palm up and away, until your palm **bone** connects to the under tip of the chin **bone**. Bullseye!!
Keep that arm driving up until it can go no further.

3) **The front or rear Head Butt.**

This is a great strike for those people who because of their size or position, find or can place their forehead or back of skull in line with their attacker's chin **bone**.

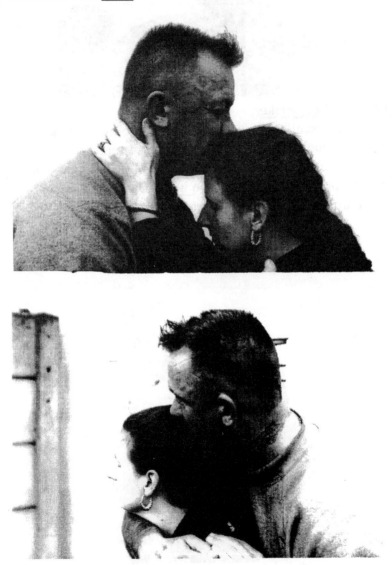

4) **The Shoulder Butt**.
This strike is useful if you are close enough to be grabbed.

You can also inflict serious damage to your assailant's lower jaw and teeth with this one.

Just pull your attacker's head down towards your shoulder and, simultaneously, drive your shoulder **bone** forward to meet his chin **bone**. Bingo!!

You must take care with this strike not to miss with your shoulder, connecting instead with your collar bone. The collar bone is quite weak and a blow to it may break or cause a fracture that will incapacitate both your arms, leaving you easy prey.

5) **The Elbow strike**.

The elbow is a devastating weapon. If you raise your hand and place it behind your own neck, you will notice your elbow sticking out in front of you. This movement, at speed, is called the rising elbow strike. If this strike forcibly connects to your attacker, under his chin **bone**, he is finished.

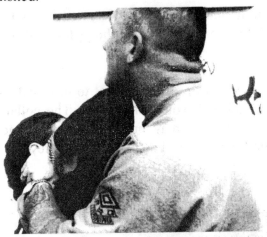

6) **The reverse elbow strike**

Also a solid weapon, to be used if the attack comes from behind.
Lift your right arm up and touch your left shoulder with the finger tips of your right hand. Your right elbow will be pointing out in front of you

Now drive your elbow backwards while pivoting on your hips.
If the **bony** tip of your elbow connects to your attacker's chin **bone**, the attacker is history.

There are a number of other possible weapons I could describe, but I think these examples are enough for you to get the idea. This is not intended to be a book of techniques

It does not matter which of the strikes you choose, so long as you are fast enough and you make a forceful connection between the **bony** weapon of your choice and your assailant's chin **bone**.

Here is a point that I want to emphasise. It is the reality of the weapon being **solid bone** that allows it to work, and not the actual body weapon that matters. To complete the link the **bony weapon must make forceful contact with the chin bone**, giving a 'bone to chin' Knockout.

Try this exercise to experience the truth of this for yourself.

Draw your tongue back into your mouth, clench your teeth together and cover your chin with one hand. Arrange for a **good** trusted friend of yours to strike the tip of your chin, protected by your own hand, fairly fast, from a couple of inches back with a solid fist.

Not too hard though, you could find your legs will turn to jelly even from this short distance.

(Ask somebody to stand behind you just in case).

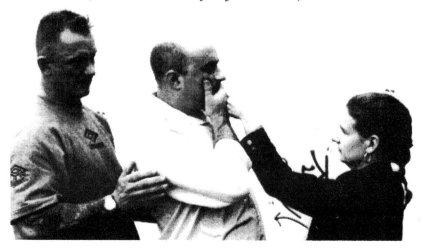

Now, try to imagine the effect of this strike if used at full strength and speed, as your Pre-emptive strike.

How could such a simple and devastating method of **knocking out an attacker** have fallen by the wayside?

Some fighting arts chose not to include such strikes and withdrew themselves from reality. The moment. Karate, Kung Fu and other kick punch arts focused on sport fighting, which maintained strict non-contact rules regarding fist to face strikes. The effectiveness of such strikes were soon forgotten.

Western Boxing also divorced itself from the old bare knuckle fighting style when padded gloves totally eliminated the effect of bone to chin bone contact.

The method ceased to exist and this stopped other bone to chin techniques from being developed.

So, if you are searching for that magical, secret method of knocking out an assailant, this has got to be the one.

If you are slightly off target and connect with either side of the jaw line, ending at the ears, you will still be able to achieve a knock-out, but with a little more difficulty.

Dogs don't know kung fu!

The most widely used form of Personal Protection in this country is the dog. Think about it! We no longer have faith in the locks on our doors and windows as a form of protection. We do not go out to buy knives, crossbows or guns to protect ourselves. We are restricted by the Law, availability and maybe, lack of confidence regarding our courage to use such weapons. So, when we want to protect ourselves and our property we buy a dog.

Dogs are legal, can be trained in many different ways, will act on instruction and are dedicated to us.

They are able to stop the most daring criminals invading our homes, and most street attackers will not target a person out walking their dog.

Obviously I am talking here about dogs that are capable of being aggressive, nobody would buy a toothless dog for protection.

There is only one reason why anyone fears a dog and that is the dog's teeth and it's ability to bite, combined with the dog's aggression.

Dogs can be likened to four legged sharks.

We do not fear being kicked, punched, grappled to the floor or head butted by a dog.
All we fear are the dog's teeth biting into our skin.
A dog's only weapon is it's teeth.

Dogs do not know Kung Fu!!

So, what can we learn from this?

We have teeth too and from the way we have developed over time through eating, chewing, crunching and biting we have acquired a devastating weapon.

We naturally bite to protect ourselves as babies and toddlers.

On many occasions I have heard parents telling their children not to bite. Biting is such a natural response for us to make in self defence, yet it gets educated out of us except for the purposes of eating. Biting is regarded as uncivilised.
I do not share this opinion when it comes to your own self protection. For years I have taught biting as an important defence against someone who grabs you aggressively. I have had no reports of teeth biting into flesh, failing to get a result. I have much faith in the technique and there are a few people around who received a free copy of my dental imprint for choosing to restrain me against my will , and bear witness to the effectiveness of the bite!
It is also because of my faith in this technique that I am never to be seen working on night-club doors without the protection of a jacket, no matter how hot it may be. *A jacket offers the only protection I have against teeth and the other cutting or tearing weapons that may be used against me. I learnt the hard way!*

Note of caution.

Nowadays we must be aware of the risk posed by the Aids Virus.

Biting will often tear through the skin with the risk of bodily fluids being exchanged. If you are bitten by your attacker you are exposed to the same risk.

This risk should be considered along with the idea of Levels of Threat that I discussed earlier. If the threat is Simple you will not consider biting. You may not decide to bite even if the threat is Serious.

"Jennifer Chelley, 49, was jailed for 30 days after she pulled out clumps of Emma Wilkins's hair, bit her on the face, punched and smashed her head against her car bonnet after a minor traffic accident"

In a Life Threatening situation however, you have everything to gain by biting.

The aids facts you need to know

Unless you have been living on Mars for the last ten years, you will be fully aware of the tragic disease Aids/ HIV and the fear of infection. You will also know that we can contract this disease from the exchange of blood and semen whilst having sex with an infected person.

Since Aids has no known cure, we must learn about the various ways it has been or could be transmitted. Some of these you probably have never considered.

Forty-one cases have so far been established, internationally, of HIV transmission via needle stick injuries.

In a back street ghetto in America, an HIV carrier robbed victims by threatening them with a syringe, containing some of his infected blood. Some of his victims placed a higher value on their possessions than their lives and were stabbed with the needle. Such attacks could easily happen here.

An American, cut in a bus crash was infected by another injured passenger who was pinned against him.

Two football players collided, resulting in open injuries to both of them and the transmission of the disease took place.

Two men had a fist fight. During the fight one of the men received a busted nose, the other a cut lip. Their fight became a wrestling match that ended on the ground. One of the men was HIV positive and during the fight, blood to blood contact occurred. They are now both infected.

In July 1990, a dentist was demonstrated to have transmitted the infection to at least six of his patients. The transmission route was never established.

Two young boys pricked their thumbs and pressed them together to become blood brothers. One of the boys was unknowingly an HIV carrier. He infected his mate. (When I was a young boy such innocent rituals were common place).

An HIV positive female became infected by her husband who had contracted the virus from one of his secret visits to prostitutes. The wife, full of anger, decided to vent her anger on men in general by having a large number of affairs herself, to spread the virus amongst her victims.

The last example concerns an Aids victim who vowed to infect as many people as possible before he died. He claimed to have placed drawing pins on cinema seats after previously dipping the tip in to an open wound on his body. He also claimed to have used blow darts dipped in to his blood. The darts were then aimed at random on city streets. He further claimed to have sold his blood to order to individuals who had grudges against cheating partners. He told of one client who allegedly injected his partner with the blood after getting her drunk when he discovered she was having an affair.

All of the above examples are for real except two. Can you tell which of the two did not happen?

The fact is that everyone of the above examples is possible. There are many possible variations too. For your own protection, you should consider the ways you could become infected and take the necessary precautions.

I am advocating Aids awareness but remember this is different to Aids phobia. There are many innocent victims out there who should receive our care and compassion, not our rejection. Do not compare their condition with the criminals who deliberately use their disease to threaten or to harm others .

Dagenham Post November 1995
" Aids victim stabbed her lover with a syringe of HIV infected blood in the arm and buttock after being jilted, and was found guilty of attempting to inflict grievous bodily harm. "

Take another look at the above examples and imagine it being you at risk of infection, how do you now apply this to what you have decided is life threatening to you and how you thought you were going to deal with a life threatening encounter.

Jekyll and hyde syndrome

This is a story most of you will know. It tells of a respectable doctor who swallows a potion. Whenever the doctor drinks the potion, he is unknowingly changed into a violent monster who becomes a killer.

A number of men have a similar monster hidden inside them but they need no potion to release it. The monster will creep out and begin to take power and control, when the man becomes sexually aroused.

During normal lovemaking, when both partners are consenting, the monster has no need to reveal himself. However, if the male becomes aroused and the female does not consent, the monster may begin to stir. He may begin to get rough. He may pin his partner down. He may try to force his partner into unwanted sex. He may continue to force himself on to his victim until he gains satisfaction and the monster departs. The monster enjoys the power and control, it gives him what he really wants.

In the case of most men the monster is controllable, but in some cases it is not. This is why we have rapists. Some men may control this inner monster through masturbation and do not need the power and control bullshit, others will visit prostitutes, and others have complete control over how their mind allows their bodies to react to others. Some have no control over their own bodies choose to take power and control of another body.

In your relationships with men you may come across this monster at some time, possibly in a relationship that is fine, for most of the time. There may a time in your life when you are having a sexual relationship with a man and you may witness the appearance of the monster applying power and control. Simply leading a man on or flirting with him, may encourage the change to occur.

It is fine if you can understand and control the person concerned but, if you wake a monster who you cannot control, you are heading for real trouble.

Take casual encounters with guys at clubs or discos as an example.

The evening may begin well. Usually the guy will flatter you and act the real nice guy. Nothing will be too good for you. He will tell you how wonderful you are. He will say that he has never met anyone like you before. He may act the real gentleman. At the end of the evening he kindly offers to see you home.

The guy is now working to a time limit.

His fuse may be shorter than you think. His intention is to have an ejaculation, with as much assistance from you as he can get. If you are happy to consent to his plan there will be no problem and you will not get to meet the monster. However, if you are not in agreement you may witness a nasty change in character, your introduction to power and control may begin..

This may sound a little frightening to you but, believe me, this happens again and again. This is not just a story that lives in the pages of a book. This is real.

Do not take my word for it, ask around. Many women out there have been charmed by their Dr. Jekylls and have then discovered that Mr. Hyde was lurking behind the friendly exterior.

Hansel and gretel

The story goes;

"When the two children entered the forest they left a trail of bread crumbs behind them so that they could retrace their footsteps and not get lost. Unfortunately, the trail was eaten by the birds and wild animals and so the children did become lost after all."

Why do I mention this fable?

Well, there are too many cases of young girls disappearing without trace. Leaving no record of where they were going or who they were meeting. There are also cases of bodies being discovered with no clues as to their identities.

Through teaching young girls self protection I have discovered that a large number of them have, at one time or another, had a secret meeting with a boyfriend and had informed no one else as to their plan, through fear of getting in trouble by an un-approving parent, or other reasons that they may have for their secrecy. They had left no trace of their movements with friends or parents.

Some girls told me that they felt their parents were over protective towards them, and did not like the restrictions enforced on the places they could go and the people they could mix with. As a result, some girls said that they began to tell lies about where they went and with whom, in order to keep out of trouble. Without thinking they were putting themselves at serious risk.

I am against the idea of secretive meetings, but I cannot ignore the fact that they do take place. Therefore, all I can do is advise on safety.

If you are ever in such a situation and feel that your meeting has to remain a secret, you must leave a record of your movements somehow.

Think about leaving the details with a trusted friend or relative, or you could leave a note in your school bag or under your mattress, maybe on a cassette tape. It does not really matter how you do it just as long as it is clear and will not disappear like a trail of bread crumbs!! When you return home safely you can destroy the trail.

Leaving this trail also provides another safeguard if things were to get nasty with the person you were secretly meeting. Without a trail they will have complete power and control . They can do whatever they want with you.

However, if you can tell them that your movements have been recorded and you are expected back at a certain time (**yes, I am telling you to lie**) , their attitude may change and may save your life without you even knowing it.

Please take my advice unless you want to end up lost or buried in some deep, dark forest?

I think that it is a good idea if all parents encourage their kids to learn how to leave trails. Learning their own addresses and telephone numbers is a good start.

Whenever I take my own children out for the day I give each of them a business card to put in a pocket. The card has all the relevant details, such as my name, address, telephone number, mobile number etc. I also write on it information appropriate for the day in question, such as my car registration number or a local contact number.

These cards can be instantly made, by using the machines to be found in large home improvement stores, for about , £4.00 for fifty cards. Alternatively you can simply write out your own cards and photocopy them.

We all know that kids tend to get lost, it has happened to most parents, but how many parents take the simple precautions I take?

Remember, even though you may have taught your child their address and phone number, what happens if they are overcome by fear or shock and are unable to supply the details?

"A BOY of five dialled 999 and asked for an ambulance after waking up to find the his mother had been stabbed to death, outside his bedroom door. Amanda Healey, 34, died from multiple knife wounds."

Another thing to consider with children is whether or not it is wise to buy them T-shirts with their names printed on them?
This would give a stranger a name to use as an intro if they wanted to take the child away, yet if you were at a town show and lost your child, it would be easy for them to be found!

Personally I prefer the choice of not displaying their names on a T-shirt and doing my job properly as a parent, and not losing them in the first place.

The law and sexual offences

Sexual offences include Rape, Indecent Assault of both males and females, Indecency with children, Incest and Buggery. What are the differences between these sexual offences? In this book I will cover Rape, Indecent Assault and Buggery.

1. RAPE.

Rape basically meant the penetration of the vagina by the penis. However, if someone else assists the rapist by holding the victim down, they are also now guilty in Law of Rape. Rape is still deemed to have occurred even if the woman's hymen is not ruptured nor semen ejaculated. (Traditionally we have associated damage to the hymen as indicating loss of virginity.) Rape is therefore quite straight forward to determine. The vagina must have been penetrated, *no matter how slightly,* by the penis without the consent of the victim.

In theory it is possible for a girl to be the victim of Rape, yet still appear to be a virgin. This is due to the female's hymen remaining undamaged by the male's penis, possibly because it was not fully inserted into the vagina. A rape charge was once proven in just such a way.

The attacker did not fully insert his penis into his victim's vagina and then proceeded to bugger and have forced oral sex with his unfortunate victim. (At the time, Buggery was a lesser offence unlike today when, as we have seen, it is now classed as Rape if forced, but forced oral sex is still regarded as Indecent Assault.) The Defence Counsel attempted to get the charge of rape dropped because the girl's hymen had not been ruptured so, technically she could still be classed a virgin. The Court, however, made the ruling that a rape had still been committed regardless of the lack of damage to the hymen. The sad thing about this case is that, if that slight penetration had not been proven, the rapist's victim would have been subjected to Buggery and yet, Rape could not have been proven. The slight penetration made all the legal difference and this, the rapist had not taken this into consideration.

Proof of virginity always crops up in rape trials, in order to establish whether or not the victim has previously had sexual experience. The Defence will go through this procedure to try to discredit the victim. It is my opinion that this is disgusting and should never happen.

2. BUGGERY.

Rape is also judged to have occurred if Buggery is the forced sexual act. This is where a man's penis penetrates another person's anus without their consent, whether the victim be male or female. If a person consents to the act of Buggery, both parties are committing an act of Buggery.

3. INDECENT ASSAULT.

Indecent assault is a sexual act that most right minded people would find offensive, but the offence is only committed when the attacker makes some attempt to use the victim's body in some way that they do not consent to, such as oral sex, groping and forced masturbation.

For instance, if a man sat opposite a woman in a railway carriage and pulled out his penis and began to masturbate, no actual assault would have occurred. However, if the man began to make sexual requests of the woman and moved towards her, an Indecent Assault would have occurred.
Although the victim had not actually been touched, she did have reasonable co ncern for her safety and this sets the condition for the Indecent Assault to have taken place. If the man had not made an actual approach towards the woman and merely continued to masturbate, he would then have been guilty of the offence of Indecent Exposure.

This is why the police try to establish **exactly** what the offender did and said.

Our personal space

"Get out of my face!"
This is another way of saying, **"Get out of my space!"**
This is a widely used expression and one that says exactly what is meant.
Our personal space is the area into which someone has to get into for us to feel intimidated.

With you at the centre, your personal space is formed by an imaginary circle around you. Different people have different sized circles depending upon their self confidence. Most people can find their 'feel safe' personal space by clasping their hands and extending them directly forward at shoulder height.

The edge of our imaginary circle is just outside of our hands. If the circle is stepped into we may suddenly feel that our space has been invaded. We can then become aggressive or frightened, prepared to defend our territory or to run away.

If we have little confidence in our ability to defend ourselves, we can begin to fall apart when we see a real or imaginary threat a long distance away from us. I know from personal experience.

As a school boy my imaginary circle covered the area of a football pitch. I was bullied by First years when I was in the Third Year. I was definitely the school wimp. I was terrified of my own shadow.

If a bully made eye contact with me from across the other side of the school football field, I would start to panic, fearing some more bullying was on the cards.

For years I walked around feeling intimidated, uncomfortable, worried and miserable. I was convinced that if I could be seen, I could be hurt. At that moment I was a lonely child with minus zero self confidence, zero self protection knowledge and I was alone in a big bad world, I felt so vulnerable.

I tried to counter this by creating a massive gap between myself and my enemies. This did not work, so I started on my study of self protection.

I took up Judo and Karate. After a year of study my confidence began to grow. I was still being bullied, still not winning any fights, but I was not running away so much. My repertoire of punches, kicks and throws was growing and my ability to perform them, with skill, increased too. Little by little something else began to change.

My personal 'feel safe' space began to shrink. I was beginning to develop some bottle.

People could now get within a car's distance before I became twitchy.

I am not going to bore you with the whole process, but it is enough to say that it took over fifteen years to change from that frightened kid, who could be intimidated by a stare from one hundred yards away, to my present level of confidence, As a night-club doorman in London's Soho, where I come face to face with hundred's of punters each night.

Some are drunk, some are abusive, others are aggressive. I am regularly challenged to fight, threatened with beatings and death, but I rarely experience fear as I knew it as a child, and my own personal space could be defined by the space inside a telephone box.

I still get a rush of adrenaline and the shakes when certain situations go down, but I no longer mistake this feeling for fear, I now understand that this is the body's natural response to warn of danger. Once I had gained in self confidence, the feeling never left me. It has increased as time and study have passed.

I have grown to understand that no one is capable of hurting me physically (without a weapon) unless they are able to touch me. If they do, I am now quite capable of dealing with the attack and I have the power to choose which option I take.

The real test of the confidence you have in your ability to look after yourself, is defined by your **'feel safe'** space. If the space you require is **unduly large** you must ask of yourself **where you feel a personal weakness**. If you discover this weakness, seek out the means to strengthen yourself.

The problem may not actually lie in your lack of self protection knowledge or ability.

A friend of mine had the ability to tear most men apart with his bare hands and yet his 'feel safe' space was considerable. All of his self protection techniques fell apart when someone fronted him. The problem was simple to find.
My friend had a speech impediment that caused him to stutter whenever he became agitated. He would then lose every ounce of his self confidence. On my advice he sought help for this problem and his confidence grew in leaps and bounds. Just having the ability to say slowly, calmly and without stuttering " I don't want any trouble now push off before I hurt you" has given him a great boost.

Some people I know are quite skilled in self protection techniques, but they are still lacking in confidence. In their case the problem lies in a lack of assertiveness and a little training here would help them immensely.

The secret is to look at your self honestly and to seek out where exactly your lack of confidence lies. Once you have discovered this seek out the means to address the problem.

For me the answer lay in Judo and Karate, although now I shudder at some of the unnecessary things I got up to, such as knuckle push ups, board breaking, barefoot jogging etc. All that stuff is total crap to me now, but at the time it was what I needed.

So, whatever it is you require to boost your confidence do it and you will see the positive results. Remember though, that what is right for one person is not necessarily right for another. We all have different needs.

A few words of warning.

Do not become overconfident. If you start to allow people to get closer to you, you may be heading for a fall.

If, for instance you see three men standing idly on a street corner sizing you up as you are approaching, widen your circle.

You wouldn't want to pat a rattle snake on the head would you?

My own personal space has become telephone box size through necessity within my line of work rather than through choice. You will find what feels right for you as you progress.

I never forget that my day may come as it has before, I may misread the seriousness of a situation or be caught out whilst switched off and unaware, (I have to sleep sometime!!) When confidence turns into over-confidence you will pay the price within your small circle. So take note.

How our senses can create our fear

Whenever I teach my self protection classes in Girls Schools, I find that this subject is really well received. It refers to an affective learning experience that is common to us all but, for some reason we feel that we are the only person in the entire world who has experienced the phenomenon. Usually, we are too embarrassed to speak about it.

At some time in our lives we have been left at home all alone or alone in some isolated part of the house away from immediate help. Suddenly we realise our situation. *WE ARE ALONE. REALLY ALONE. NOBODY ELSE IS HERE.*

At first you felt completely safe but what if you were attacked right now? No help would be at hand, you could be raped, tortured or murdered and nobody would ever know. Fear starts to get a grip of you. It is Thriller time!!

Your mind recalls all those Horror movies that have terrified you. All those films that you were told not to watch as a kid, you get flashbacks of the Boogie man tearing the baby sitter apart. You cannot take that shower in case a Psycho appears with a knife to get you. The toy clown in the corner seems to be following your movements with it's eyes and your fear of the unknown is getting more and more of a hold on you.

You hear a noise outside the door, you see a shadow flit across the curtains. Is that a face looking through the window?

Now you are scared shitless.............

STOP! STOP! STOP!

Switch on the television, phone a friend for a chat, make yourself a cup of tea or a snack, go and check the baby you are minding. You tell yourself not to be so stupid. Good! you have got a grip on yourself again.

All is well so you can settle down to watch the TV. But now your eyes and ears have become very sensitised. The room is getting darker, just like in those Horror movies you were just thinking about. You can hear a pin drop. What is that scratching noise outside the door ? Is it coming from the wall? The light seems to dim.

You can feel a strange presence in the room that was not there before. Somebody or some thing is in the room with you.

YOU CAN HEAR BREATHING. HEAVY BREATHING. IT IS BEHIND YOU. Now your heart is racing, you are sweating, shaking, adrenaline is rushing around your bloodstream. Your feet are curled up under you in case something makes a grab for them. You want to scream. You are about to panic. You manage to control yourself. You slowly get up, you have found the courage to look behind you.
You suddenly jump around to confront the beast and surprise, surprise, there is nobody else in the room but you. Reason told you that all along, but your imagination and your senses played games with you.
So, how many times have you crept up to a cupboard door or to a set of curtains pulling them open fast because you became convinced someone was hiding? How many times have you pulled the bedcover's back in case something was underneath them, ready to grab you? I have experienced all these things and more as a child.

I am not embarrassed at all by the disclosure. We have all been there and you are no different to anyone else.
When the light starts to dim, it can play wonderful tricks on our eyes and ears. All our Affective learning which involves our feelings, attitude, and emotions comes into play.
Every branch of a tree can become a monster. Draughts that creep in through gaps in doors, windows, down chimneys and through cat flaps or letter boxes are unnoticed during day light hours.

At night they become the sounds of intruders creeping around the house.

A cat peering through your window in the day is welcomed or sent packing, but at night it may become a glaring creature from Hell waiting to pounce.

What we see and hear during daylight hours is in fact, no different in darkness. However, our logical, rational thought processes are destroyed and our senses do their best to scare us to death.

I have missed out one further part of this little drama, a part that takes a little of the fear away. A small comfort.

 *Before you crept into the hall to confront your imaginary fiend from Hell you suddenly became an expert in the use of every day items as effective weapons.*

You were able to pick up the T.V remote control, a newspaper, a telephone, a cup, a plate, a nappy pin, or a poker to use as a deadly weapon against your adversary.

With no time for logical thought we naturally grab the first thing that comes to hand, with no idea either, regarding how we intend to use the weapon.

Because we are frightened and we are not sure what we are about to face, we reach for some kind of back-up. We do this by simulating possession of a real weapon by picking up the nearest thing to hand.

We have now demonstrated our natural willingness to use a real weapon in order to survive. We may as well make use of this willingness by learning how to use such every day items as really effective weapons. (see the section entitled **'The Twentieth Century's most secret weapons.'**)

In the girls school classes I hold, I think I have heard of every possible item that has been grabbed to protect themselves against nothing more than their imaginations. As a matter of interest, none of the girls that I have taught has actually come face to face with anybody in one of these situations.

However, if The Queen can wake up to find an intruder in her bedroom we cannot dismiss the possibility of it happening to us.

The closest any one of my students came to such an unpleasant encounter was when two of the girls were playing records upstairs in a bedroom whilst home alone. When the parents returned home after their night out they discovered that intruders had broken in downstairs and the house had been burgled. The two girls had heard nothing. It is frightening to think what could have happened.

On a lighter note, here is a list of some of the 'weapons' the girls have admitted to 'arming' themselves with:

The pet cat - Knitting needles - goldfish bowl including goldfish

hot drink - hockey stick - hairbrush - pair of scissors - Ornaments

hair drier - stiletto shoe - fly spray - ornamental sword - nappy pin

What have you grabbed as your weapon?

What did you seriously intend to do with it?

Do not think up a clever technique now that time has passed. Think back to the moment. What were you honestly going to do with this 'weapon' that you had never considered as a weapon before?

You must admit that you have ignored the possibility that a real attack could occur in your home just as we have established that it could happen to you on the street, or in the park. That is why you have taken no measures to arm your self with any relevant self protection knowledge.

You are still no more capable at the present moment in time, than you were the last time you quickly pulled the bed covers back as a small child. However, today you are making progress by getting this far in my book.

You did not realise that raising your awareness could be so informative and stimulating did you? Please read on now that you have got this far.

Learn from the experience of others and do not become another sad statistic.

Strange but true:-

"Pc Stephen Dunsdon, was convicted of a road rage attack on a woman while he was on his way to Buckingham Palace. Dunsdon, who guarded the Queen's bedroom was once commended for disarming a deranged knifeman at the Palace."

Shocking the body

The Oxford Dictionary defines shock as follows:

'The effect of a violent impact or shake; A sudden violent effect upon the mind or emotions; An acute state of prostration caused by physical injury.'

Anyone in the medical profession will tell you, that there is no cure for shock. The treatment needs to be aimed at the underlying cause of the shock, rather than at the shock itself.

However, knowing the serious effect that shock has on the body, we can take advantage of this if our safety is threatened by an attacker. What effect will shock have on our attacker?

Shock will temporarily freeze your attacker's body movement which interrupts their planned strike. Their brain will be uncontrollably engaged by a kind of mental wipe out, everything will go blank for a few moments.
The attacker will become disoriented and incapable of focusing his eyes. His attack or defence capability will be considerably reduced.
His brain will then register that he has received a hit and he will need a few seconds to assess the level of damage, before he can continue.
Effectively the attacker will become a vulnerable rag doll incapable of imposing a threat for a few vital seconds. These are the few seconds that you are looking for, they could be vital for your survival.

But why worry about shocking our attacker when we could simply take them out with our trusty Pre-emptive strike?

Of course, if you are in the position to knock your attacker out immediately and the level of threat justifies this, do it. However, this may not always be the case, for no matter how effective we think our self protection skills may be we will, one day, meet an attacker who breaks through our ring of confidence.

Their size, manner, voice or reputation will intimidate us and our bottle will start to disappear. This is exactly the point at which you will need a chance. An equaliser. You urgently need to freeze your assailant's body so you can run away or strike a blow. Your ability to cause shock to your attacker's system will be this equaliser.

So, how do we generate shock to the attacker's body?

One of the most simple method's is a **hard, fast palm slap across the side of attacker's face**.

I am not talking here about the common slap around the jaw using only the inner fingers.

I mean using the complete area of the hand i.e. the area of the hand that would be in contact with the floor in a push up position.

This would feel like a shovel striking the side of the head and with trained use of the turning hips, can be devastating. Some people I know, have perfected this strike to such an extent that they use it as their Pre-emptive strike.

I am not going to explain the detailed body mechanics needed for this strike because this is not a book on physical training. I simply want you to understand how it is possible to shock the attacker's body.

Most people will under estimate the power of the palm slap until they are on the receiving end of one. So, give this exercise a try.

Place the flat of your hands on each side of your neck. Your finger tips should be wrapped around your neck meeting at the vertebrae. Get your trusted friend to slap their open hands down onto your hands as they would if performing loud clapping. **Both palms must make contact with a respectable level of force simultaneously in order for the effect to be experienced.**

Now that you have had a taster, imagine being an attacker with a set plan of attack, usually beginning with a verbal introduction designed to suss you out before he hits, but suddenly out of nowhere, his body receives a stunning shock, **BANG!!**

His body will be frozen, he is confused and now he is completely open to attack. Look at the time it took for you to recover in the little exercise when you were expecting the slap.

The experience you felt was with the added protection from your hands and the slap would not have been full force, unless your partner was not the friend you believed them to be.

Imagine how a full force, unexpected, double handed palm slap would feel to the unprotected area of the head or the neck. It is truly devastating.

A rolled newspaper used as a striking tool, in the manner of a powerful tennis stroke, to the same area of the body will achieve a similar effect.

If your shocking effect is developed and can be combined with your Pre-emptive strike, you will be a force to be reckoned with.

A double knife-hand strike with your palms face up and your wrist bones driving into the side of your attacker's head or neck, launched in the same manner as the double slap, is an example of such a weapon.

There are more. Try to think of some.

Self protection or martial art?

The term Martial Art describes fighting techniques that were ***proven in battle*** centuries ago in the East. Using this classification Self Protection becomes a modern Martial art only when it becomes tried and tested in combat itself.

A truly effective Self Protection system designed to cope with the present, rather than the past is closer to the ideal of a Martial Art than most of the 'Martial Arts' taught today.

The traditional Martial Arts have become redundant in modern warfare, largely having been replaced by guns, planes and technology.

There is no longer a great need to be able to punch through the wooden armour of a Samurai warrior or to fight with a sword whilst on horseback.

On the streets, we are now faced with steel toe cap boots, knives, bottles, being glassed or raped. The enemy's reasons and methods of attack today are not comparable to those of the Eastern fighters of old.

Sadly, most people involved in the Martial Arts today are blind to the fact that a modern threat demands a modern response.

Teaching the traditional Martial Arts systems as self protection today is largely done as a matter of habit and does not relate to their practical effectiveness on the streets.

I can hear the outcry from the defenders of these Arts already.

They will proclaim that their kicks, chops, punches, blocks and throws are devastating. Yeah! It will be true that they can select some effective techniques from their systems.

However, **if you study these same systems you will find large areas that are of no use whatsoever in Self protection.**

Instructors of this type of training must know this to be a true fact and that many of the techniques they are teaching have no place against the modern attacker on the streets of our cities.

However these systems continue to be taught, still promoting many useless movements and female students are led to believe that they are being shown how to protect themselves.
Rubbish!!

You must realise what such people refuse to accept.

The traditional Martial arts are
"History passed down in physical form" snippets of a bygone age.

We don't try to speak like Samurai Warriors so why try to fight like them?

To arrive at the few effective techniques you will have to practice a large percentage of rubbish. What a waste of time and effort.

Just because you could take a kick from football and use it for self protection, do you have to learn all the other skills of the sport to stay safe on the streets?

If you decide to try out your local Martial arts club, ask the instructor questions that you need answers to, After all you would do the self same thing if you were learning to drive and wanted to know that you were in good hands.

" What can you teach me that will raise my awareness on the streets? What can you teach me about threat evaluation? How can I avoid becoming another Rape statistic? What would be a suitable practical pre-emptive strike for me to practice? Which part of your system has specifically been designed to deal with rape?"

 Their answers should tell you whether to enrol or to try some place else.

If you want to practice the traditional Martial Arts for their historical content, fitness, discipline or to meet new friends and improve your social life that's fine.

These Arts can provide all these benefits and they have my respect for this. However, if you want to learn effective, practical Self Protection you will have to look elsewhere, to avoid wasting a lot of your valuable time and energy.

Instructors of true self protection are around if you care to search and know what you are looking for.

The twentieth century secret weapon

The Law does not allow us to carry weapons. Even though attackers carry and use weapons the Law still only allows us to use reasonable force in self defence, this leaves **us** empty handed. We are left with our skin and bone against the attacker's *broken bottle, knife, knuckle duster, brick, baseball bat etc.*

The Law does not seem to provide us with adequate protection **and the attacker is fully aware of this advantage**.

If you think that weapons are hard to get hold of, because they are illegal, consider the photograph below.

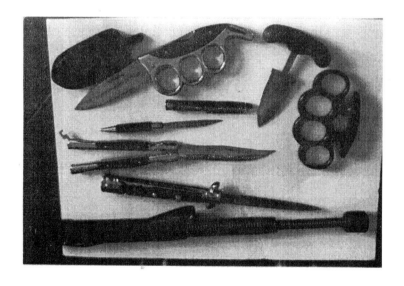

All of these weapons were actually carried by one person, in a gift wrapped box not much bigger than the size of a video cassette and taken into a club looking like a birthday present.

The box contained a knuckle duster, a knuckle duster with a locking blade, a telescopic baton, a flick knife, a pen with a hidden blade, a balisong or butterfly knife, and a belt knife.

Imagine the damage that these weapons could cause in the hands of six thugs. In total the weapons cost just seventy pounds. So, you can see how easy it is for weapons to get into the wrong hands.

We would be prosecuted if we carried a knife for our own self protection.
The law only allows us to carry a **folding pocket knife with a blade of less than three inches not carried or used for self defence, yet a child of just fifteen years old can be granted a shot gun licence!!**

We have already realised and accepted that as a reaction to fear, *we will grab anything that comes to hand to protect ourselves*, without any thought of the Law or how we actually intend to use the weapon. (See the section called ' **How our senses can create our fear.**')

Maybe it is about time we looked at legal possibilities that will balance the scales when protecting ourselves.

As a young Black Belt I received plenty of weapon training, but I soon realised that none of this was of any real use to me, because I could never legally carry these same weapons. So, I gave up practising weapons completely.
Shortly after, I was invited by the Japanese Jujitsu and Karate military section to teach my Self protection art to their instructors and students at a course in Southampton as a guest instructor. It was there that I witnessed my friend and fellow Self Protection instructor Dave Tourton demonstrate a most amazing skill from his Ju jitsu system, where he could have attackers screaming for mercy using only a small pencil sized piece of wood.

All my years of training in the Martial Arts, including weaponry, had not impressed me half as much as the lethal use of this innocent looking, pencil-shaped piece of wood.

The system Dave had demonstrated fifteen years ago was called Yawara bo, meaning Short Stick. Dave taught me the basic skills of the Short Stick and this has stayed with me to this day.

Now I teach it as part of my own Self Protection programme.

Over a period of time I found that I was able to apply the basics of short stick training to other items such as pencils, pens, remote controls, combs, Aluminium pocket and keyring torches etc.
Infact, I soon realised that these basics applied to countless everyday items.
I even managed to fine tune this art to enable me to gain release from an attacker using only a folded piece of paper.
I now have weapons all around me for instant use if ever the need arises.
This weapon use ability has to be one of the most well kept secrets of using **non weapons as weapons** in order to survive.

We are surrounded by scores of weapons as long as we know how to use them effectively. Can you imagine a young woman being prosecuted for stopping a rapist by defending herself with a pocket calculator, a teaspoon, a newspaper or a floppy disc?

As I am writing this I know that you are thinking that I have finally lost my mind big time. You don't believe a word of this, do you?

All I can say is that these short stick skills are for real. I know that you have probably heard the usual tips, such as digging a bunch of keys into an attacker's face or throwing some loose change into his eyes, but these short stick skills are different.

Give the training a few hours of your time and you will never be without an effective weapon for the rest of your life. Furthermore you will be unable to resist demonstrating your new skill to friends on every available occasion.

For the purpose of explaining the basics, I will simply use a pen or pencil as this is the most common and widely available item. There will be no need for you to learn the multiple ways to hold the pen to transform it into a weapon, instead I will show you four easy to remember grips that you will never forget.

Picture 1. **The Pointing Finger Grip**.

Method: Use as a simple extension of your forefinger. Grip between your forefinger and thumb. Strike with the point as in the fingertip jab.

Target areas: Eyes, throat, chest plate, face etc.

Weapon items: Pen, pencil, slimline remote, floppy disc corner, packet of hard roll sweets, keys, bottom of Aluminium pocket torch, school compass, ruler, corner of a cassette or C.D case, corner tip of mobile phone battery, tooth picks, etc.
Weaker items for eye strikes can include a creased tip of a bent drinking straw, lolly stick, matchsticks, credit card corner, hard corner tip of paper folded to its maximum, lipstick container and so on.

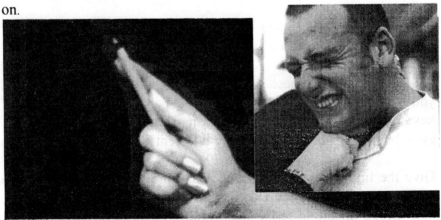

Picture 2. **The Cigarette Lighter Grip.**

Method: All four fingers wrapped around the pencil, the thumb resting on the pencil top. Target areas can then be trapped between pencil top and thumb, to grind, squeeze, pull or twist the loose flesh.

Target areas: Ear, eyelids, cheeks, neck, nose or loose fleshy areas.

Weapon items: Pen, pencil, roll sweets, lolly stick, hard corner tip of paper, bottom of Aluminium pocket torch, ruler, nail file, tea spoon, clothes peg, toothbrush handle tip, disposable razor tip, small open ended spanner etc.

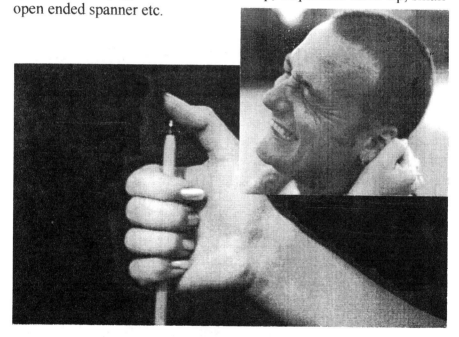

Picture 3. **Palm Push Grip.**

Method: Item is held between the little finger and the thumb, driving the hand forward as in a palm heel strike. (some weapons allow you to also scrape across target)

Target areas: Eyes, nose, lips, chin, face or throat.

Weapon items: Multi-tipped scalp massage brush, Prong tips of a household mains plug, middle of Aluminium pocket torch, edge of food tins, mobile phone, cassette tape etc.

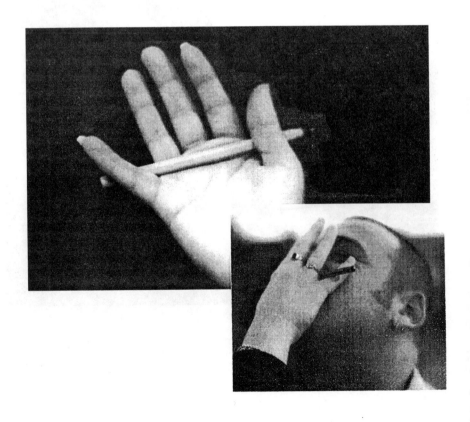

Picture 4. **Hammer Strike Grip.**

Method: Hold item in your fist and lock with the thumb. Strike with the end opposite the thumb.

Target areas: Temple, side of the neck, eyes, face, chest plate, shoulder muscles, ear.

Weapon items: bottom of Aluminium pocket torch, corner tip of slimline remote, tip of compass, tip of ruler, tip of pen or pencil, cutlery, tip of toothbrush handle, tip of disposable razor handle, tip edge of mobile phone or battery, packet of roll sweets etc.

As you can see, **the list of possible objects that can be used as a weapon in self protection are limitless**.

It is practically impossible to be in any environment without having some object within reach that could be used in self defence.

The great thing about all the items I have listed is that **none of them are weapons by design**, they have not been converted in any way to be used as a weapon and they are not banned by law.

You still have no right in law to use any weapon to protect yourself but, taking all things into consideration, it would not be judged unjust by right minded people, if you were to defend yourself against attempted strangulation by hammer fisting the corner of your mobile phone into the attacker's eye.

Consider how different this outcome may have been?

Gisela Braun realised that she had just hitched a lift from the " Devil's Moor Murderer " and was about to become his 13th victim. One of his previous victims was strangled & stabbed 57 times. Gisela was not skilled in the Martial Arts or any other type of Self Defence system, but she knew clearly that her life was at stake.

She decided to stall for time, knowing every second Could have been her last. In reply to being told to strip, she said to the attacker, "I don't mind doing it with you, but I'm a bit worked up. Let me smoke a cigarette first. It always gets me in the mood."

The Devils Moor murderer thought that she was not aware of who he was or what he was about to do to her, so he did not hesitate to light up her cigarette. Gisela took a long drag on the cigarette until the end glowed red, then with a quick movement, pressed it into the man's left eye.

He screamed in pain as he clutched his face, while she tripped the door handle, sprang out of the car and ran off into the dark. As he switched on his lights to try to find her, she read his lighted number plate and scratched the registration into the earth.

The result was she survived and he was traced the next day and was subsequently sentenced to confinement for the remainder of his life, in an institution for the criminally insane.

The whole result was due to a cigarette being used as a weapon. Just think about it.

Have a think about everyday items that you have always carried around with you, in your bag, in your car, for use in school, work, home or for social events. You will now see a wealth of weaponry at your command that you would never have considered before reading this book.

Always make sure that you are not carrying or using banned deterrents like CS Gas, Pepper sprays, Stun Guns etc.. They are banned in the U.K.

If attacked indoors, you have many household products that will stop somebody who is intent on raping you.

I'm pretty sure that if I attacked you and you responded by emptying a cup of bleach into my eyes, or a packet of Cyan & Paprika, I would be doing a quick U turn out the door.

I even know one girl who had stripped down one of those electronic hand held gas ignition lighters used for lighting up cookers, and made a convincing stun gun lookalike.
In the dark it looked pretty convincing as a deterrent to would be peeping toms, although in reality it would have been useless. The slight adaptation of a pocket flash camera would do the real damage but that's not what I want you to do. I just want to raise your awareness of the resources that are really available to you in order to save the **one life** that you have.

Deceive the mugger

Mugging is common and rife in certain areas. All the average mugger wants are tradable goods or money.

When confronted by a mugger, you are faced with the following decision:

1. *Hand over your purse containing your money, keys, travel card, phone cards etc.*
2. *Put up a fight in order to keep your valuables.*

Which would you choose?

Neither option appeals to me because both ways you lose.

Option 1. *The loss is obvious.*

Option 2. *You intentionally place your own personal safety at risk to protect materialistic items that can be replaced. Is it worth risking your life for metal, plastic and paper? You'd be crazy to try.*

If you had to chose one of the above options, then I think option 1 is the best choice, as it is the lesser of the two evils. **Personally I prefer a third option.**

Option 3

Once again we hit on the word *__deception.__* Is the message getting through yet?

Deception is a weapon that we can use in various ways in self protection. How do we apply it here?

You give the mugger exactly what he wants but, actually, you are giving him nothing at all. *__You give him a dummy purse or wallet which you substitute for the real thing. To all intent and purposes it is the real thing.__*

Get yourself an old purse. They can be picked up for pennies at a boot sale. Fill it with coins to the value of a few pounds. Add some old house keys that no longer fit any locks, some used phone cards, useless business cards and anything else to add some authenticity.

The idea is that when challenged to give up your real purse, you get out and open the dummy one, throw it in the opposite direction to which you are able to run. The coins will scatter, the mugger will go for the purse, grab it and run. You will be off and away with your real valuables safe and sound.

One of my teenage students used my dummy purse idea successfully, when she was confronted by three girl bullies whilst she was out shopping for her Grandmother. She had her Grandmother's weekly shopping allowance on her at the time. She threw the dummy purse, avoided a possible beating by giving the bullies the satisfaction that she had surrendered her valuables and actually she had given them nothing. If she hadn't used the dummy purse a lot of suffering and stress would have been caused by the robbery. Instead the stress was minimised and the bullies were reported to the police.

The dummy purse is not the ultimate solution in dealing with all muggers but I bet it's an option that you had never considered. It is also another step along the way to understanding Self Protection as the prevention rather than Self Defence as the cure.

The 5 year diary

At the beginning of each new Self Protection course that I run, I tell my students, that if they have any questions to ask that they do not want the class to share, they are welcome to talk to me after the class is over.

On one occasion a young girl approached me when the other students had left and the hall was empty. The girl was nervous and her voice was quivering. After a couple of deep breaths she said that a friend of hers had a serious personal problem and she wondered if I could offer some advice to take back to her friend. I was pretty sure that the young girl was actually talking about herself but couldn't bring herself to talk in these terms.

The story was *that her 'friend' suddenly started to receive the unwelcome attention of an adult family friend*. This started when the girl was just 12 years old.

This older man was apparently highly respected in the local community and very influential. Her parents thought a lot of this man and often invited him into the family home. On a couple of occasions the man had fondled the girl and then his approaches became more regular. The girl had told her parents but they had disregarded her story, probably out of deference either to the man's good name or to his power in the community.

My student asked me what her 'friend' could now do?

I advised her to tell the police, a teacher or any other trusted person who would act on her 'friend's' behalf. I offered help myself. "No", my student said, because her 'friend' would never risk destroying her family. She would never forgive herself if this became public.

She asked me if I had any other suggestions.

My only advice to her was to tell her 'friend' to keep a 5 year diary. Her 'friend' should first tell everybody in her life, including the male abuser, that she was starting such a diary and that it was going to include everything that happens in her life from the day she begins to write it.
She was to carry the diary with her at all times, no matter where she went. Of course, the diary could get mislaid and the finder might read the entries!!
Abuse that happened to the youngster when she was twelve would still be there on paper 5 years later when the girl would be seventeen.
Nobody thinking logically would want anything of this nature to be recorded in a diary that would still be available 5 years later. This would hopefully provide a measure of protection to the abused girl.

The girl did in fact start her diary and informed her abuser what she was doing. I met the same girl when she was sixteen when she thanked me for the advice I had offered . She admitted that it had been her who really had the problem and told me that the diary had worked and she had never been touched by this man again. She also told me that she had passed this information on to a couple of her friends who had similar problems and in each case the diary had done the trick.

Personally, I would have been happier if the abusers had been reported, but the diaries did seem to have ended a number of cases of sexual abuse.

I would always advise a child who could not or would not, for whatever reason, report their abusers, to try this method. It may not bring the abuser to justice but it may cut the abuse short.

Dealing with cars that stop pedestrians

How often have you been called over to a car to give directions?
I think it must have happened to all of us at some time in our lives.
Equally, most of us who drive have stopped and asked directions whilst out driving.
Genuine people that need directions should know better than to ask young children or women to come over to a car for directions. A motorist should try to realise just how frightening and intimidating this could be.
If we were not such polite people we could counter this problem quite easily by saying *" go buy yourself a map."* However we tend not to be like that and due to this, we leave ourselves vulnerable when cars do approach us.
Consider the following case:-

" I was waiting outside the shop for my boyfriend to arrive. A car pulled up and the passenger held out some type of map, asking where they were on the map. I wanted to get rid of them before my boyfriend arrived just in case he got the wrong idea and started trouble.
I went to the car to show where we were on the map. Suddenly the passenger grabbed my hair and screamed at me to get in. I screamed and fought. The car pulled off and the guy kept hold of my hair.
I was dragged the length of the street and the skin of my legs and hands were taken down to the bone. The car sped off and I was laying there until the ambulance was called sometime later. It all happened so fast I cannot remember the car or the attackers. I thought I was going to die."

Here is another example:-
" A car pulled up to ask me directions. It was a single female driving so I thought nothing of it. She opened the passenger door and leant across to call me. She said the window didn't work.
As I approached the car and bent over to speak to her I was pushed from behind into the car and a weapon was put to my back. It was a man's voice and he told me to shut up and I wouldn't get hurt. They Drove me away and took all my money and my jewellery off me. They took my home address off of my driving licence and said that if I ever reported the robbery to the police they would have somebody pay me a visit. I was just glad to get away."

This final example featured on the Crimewatch Programme on T.V:-

A pensioner was asked by a young lady if he knew where a vet could be found because her dog had been injured. The victim Said that he could direct her to a vets. Firstly the woman asked him if he could look at the condition of the injured dog who was in the back of her van. As he looked a man grabbed him from inside the van, pulled him in and the pensioner was driven off. He was robbed of his pension money that he had just collected and stabbed twice before being thrown from the moving vehicle.

All of the examples above are real and many more could be found. So, please never go over to any stranger's car for any reason.

If you do happen to notice a car that is acting in a strange manner, take down the details and phone the police or, if you really feel threatened by the car and there is no one else around , take down the details and post them through a handy letter box. Leave nothing to chance and ***do not take risks just to appear polite.***

The telephone and self protection

Without a doubt the telephone is the best method we have of keeping in contact when we have to travel away from home. However, is very common for us to be travelling without the necessary change for the phone and of course there will never be anyone around with change when we need it. You may think the answer is simple-**reverse the charge**, but things are often not that simple. How many cab companies do you know who will accept a reverse charge call?

The answer is virtually none. Many of the school girls who I have taught over the years have told me that their parents would not accept a reverse charge call at any time. Personally, I find that attitude very worrying when the call could relate to a real emergency.

So, is there a solution? Yes, it's called the **British Telecom Charge Card.**

How do you get one? What is the cost? How do they work?

All you need to do is to call **FREE***fone* **0800 800 893** and BT will send you an application form. Once you get the form you will need to write down your name, choose your own 4 digit pin number and fill in your name, address and home phone number. If you are under 18 years old the person paying for the bill will have to apply for you. The next choice that you have to make is which of the following options you require:-

1. International direct calls within the UK and to and from Abroad.
2. National direct calls only within the UK.
3. Phone home calls which allow calls to one phone number only, usually your own

I suggest that if your child is ever likely to be away from home alone or even if they are travelling with friends they should be carrying a card that **allows the third option as a minimum**.

__The card costs nothing__, it cannot be abused by anyone who does not know the pin number and best of all the it isn't even necessary to be carrying the card providing the pin number is remembered.

Most adults can recall their National Insurance number so children should be able to remember their card pin numbers. If they did have difficulty remembering the number it could always be written on the back of their watch straps or inside a shoe etc.

Another good reason for using a charge card is that it is cheaper than the call charges of a pay phone plus, you don't have to be embarrassed to ask to use somebody else's phone because the call will cost them nothing.

There is one disadvantage with this and that is that you cannot use the card on or apply for the card to charged to any line that is not a B.T line. So, if you have a Cable or Mercury line at home you will have to get someone else who has a B.T line to apply for you.

Whilst on the subject of telephones let's cover some other things:-

You should __learn to use your phone to dial the emergency services with your eyes closed__. Emergencies can just as easily happen in the dark as they can in the light.

Many, professional burglars will remove light bulbs when they go through a house. By doing this it is not possible for anyone arriving home to instantly see who and what is going on. If you were upstairs and you heard an intruder downstairs, you would be more sensible to call the police without drawing attention to yourself by switching on lights.

If you have a telephone with a telephone number storage facility it would be a good idea to store the 999 number on a single touch button. This would be easy for you to use in the dark and easier for a child to use in an emergency.

Another idea worth considering is the use of a code word to let someone know you are having a problem. This code word could be used over the phone only in emergencies and would immediately indicate to the person receiving the call that the caller was in trouble.

An example of this would be if a child called home and called his father by his first name or daddy when he would normally be called dad. This would alert the father that their was a problem without alerting the people listening to the child's conversation.

If a female was being beaten by a partner and needed help from a brother or friend without having the phone snatched away she could mention 'Granddad's birthday' or ask " are you still coming over for that video tape?"
It does not matter which code that you use as long as the person receiving the call recognises and acts on it. You can even alert someone by ringing their number twice and then putting the phone down. They can then phone 1471 if they have a B.T line and recognise your number. The list of codes and their uses are endless. However be sure to use a simple one and never let anyone misuse the code as a joke. **It must be reserved for real emergencies only.**

Malicious Calls.

The worst thing about the unwanted call is that the person making that call has entered your home uninvited. They may not have come in through the front door but they have got in. They have got in because they know that you will answer the phone. Remember though, you are the one in control.

The type of call can be indecent, menacing or simply annoying. So, how do you deal with these calls?

Keep calm and never show any emotion. Do not give them the pleasure of knowing that they are having any effect on you. Never give your name or telephone number when answering your phone just say "Hello". The same applies to your answer phone if you have one. If you are asked your number do not give it, just ask the caller which number they want. After all they should know which number they dialled. Make sure that the other members of your family follow the same procedure.

Never advertise the fact on your answer-phone that you are away from home for the weekend, or will not be home until a certain time. If you do advertise your absence you are unwittingly inviting people to rob your home or lay in wait for you to return.
Just leave an answer phone message that says that you are unable to take calls at the moment. Another sensible precaution is to limit the amount of information you give in your phone directory entry, give no clues.
Do not give your Marital status or first name, keep it simple such as J.O'Keefe. By doing this anyone scanning the phone book for single women to call will not find you.

If you do get a malicious call put the phone down. If the phone rings again do not speak, just wait. If it is a friend they will speak first. If it is the same malicious caller put the phone onto a cushion or chair and leave it a few minutes before replacing the hand set.

If you are not in the U.K. *(I say this because its illegal to record or monitor other peoples conversations without their permission, also its an offence to connect non-approved equipment to a rented Telecom line, although its not illegal to buy and own such equipment.)*

You could always record the caller with a simple telephone recording device, which sticks onto the back of the ear piece by a rubber suction pad while the other end plugs into the micro phone input of a Dictaphone or Mono cassette recorder.

Try not to use a Stereo recorder because the results are poor because the caller will only be recorded on one channel with lots of interference when you play it back. These recording devices are available from the major electrical goods store Tandy for around £3.00.

Some modern answer-phones have a recording facility But these usually bleep every few seconds which will, alert the caller to the fact that they are being recorded. I am only recommending recording malicious calls not every day conversations which would be taking advantage of your regular callers.

If the malicious calls continue you can report these problems to B.T and the police and show them your previously taped calls. B.T have a specially trained team that works with the police. Together they can trace almost all malicious calls whether they originate from public, private or mobile phones anywhere in the country.

Unfortunately, at the moment of writing, B.T. do not have the provision where you can automatically refuse to accept calls where the 141 code has been dialled to stop their number being detected. Mercury offer such a service and may be the solution to your problem.

If you are having a problem with malicious calls you can get free advice from a recorded message on **FREE***fone* **0800 666 700** or you can speak to someone in person between
8 am - 6 pm Monday to Saturday by dialling 150. This call is also free.

If the calls are causing you serious problems just phone your nearest B.T. bureau on **FREE***phone* **0800 661 441** during office hours.

Finally you could consider changing your phone number or becoming ex-directory.

Self protection without the use of your eyesight

Your wealth of knowledge and physical abilities can become redundant within seconds if, for any reason, you lose the use of your eyes, you will lose your bearings, your sense of direction and you will feel instant vulnerability. You will be lost in a situation that will feel totally unfamiliar.

An un-sighted person would be more able to defend themselves because, for them, the situation would be normal and familiar. For a sighted person, however, a sudden loss of sight would result in a dramatic and shocking change.

Here are a few examples of how this could happen

1. Sand, dirt or dust thrown into the eyes just before an attack.
2. A bag or hood thrown over the head.
3. A strike to the eyes e.g. fingertip jab, beer glass.
4. Liquids into the eyes e.g. Ammonia. Bleach, Acid, Nicotine saliva (Spit).
5. Powder products like salt, pepper, flour or sugar.
6. Household products such as Ant or Weed killer, powder cleaners, washing powder.
7. Aerosols e.g. polish, Air freshener, fly spray or oven cleaners.
8. Sudden power cuts resulting in total darkness.
9. Suddenly being woken at night and having no time to become adjusted to darkness.
10. Bright light being shone directly into the eyes.
11. Attacker's hands covering the eyes usually from behind.
12. Loss of glasses or contact lenses.
13. Smoke filled room or smoke blown into the eyes.
14. A blow to the head.
15. A blind fold.
16. Continuous sneezing after the nasal inhalation of an irritant like pepper.

It is a useful exercise to get to know your home surroundings with your eyes closed in order to practice escaping an attack or seeking help. Learn to find and open the front door, open a window, use the telephone or find a weapon without looking.

Outside your home such practice could be very unsafe when performing such things as running.

Self Protection relies heavily on the use of eyesight, especially when we use physical techniques. With practice, these same techniques can be re-learnt or adjusted so that they can work without the use of the eyes.

The easiest way to begin to re-learn is in the standing grappling position i.e. by standing very close to your partner and grabbing them round the neck or by the shoulder or arm. By practising in this standing grappling range, with your eyes closed, you are simulating an attack that has caused you to lose the use of your eyesight. You can be sure that if an attacker has gone to the extreme of taking away your eyesight, even temporarily, he means business.

Our three choices in self protection

1. Use our prior existing knowledge and abilities.
2. Use our new found theoretical knowledge and practical abilities.
3. Do nothing at all.

Using existing knowledge and abilities.

This area draws on all our past experiences. Men normally have experiences of schoolboy fights, sometimes gang fights, fights at football matches, participating in the fighting arts or spectating. However, females seem to have much less, if any, real experience of fighting to draw on. Boxing, schoolgirl fights, gang fights etc. are not really a part of their growing up. Things may be different for the girl gangs in the American Bronx but that is not where we are.

Females here tend to spend more time developing their academic, social and domestic knowledge through study and practice. The nearest they usually come to having any prior knowledge that they can draw on in self protection is, the secret that is not a secret i.e. *'kick him in the balls'* covered earlier.

At a push some but very few women will have practised some Judo, Karate, Kung Fu etc. but will never have been able to convert these physical skills to self protection unless the attack is Pre-arranged, which of course it will never be.
A handful now practice the western boxing style of aerobic workout and of course we have female Kickboxing and Thai boxing champions who practice using hard face contact. But these are very dedicated and special individuals. So, all in all, the average female does not tend to have any existing prior knowledge or ability that she can draw on to help her avoid a dangerous situation or an attacker.

Using new found theoretical knowledge and practical skills

This is where people like myself come in.

This book and my personal teaching courses will aim to supply you with self-protection knowledge in both the theory and the practical skills.
The knowledge will based on life as it is today and how to skilfully apply it so it will be effective.

I have one aim only which is to provide you with the information that will help you to **assess, evaluate and avoid** a situation of possible danger.

If you are unable to avoid the situation and are forced to deal physically with an attacker, my instruction will give you a back up system of weaponry that will allow you to look after yourself.

I have no intention of making you look good in your techniques or to win trophies in a sports arena.
I simply want to help you to survive a confrontation if your back is up against the wall and there is no way out other than to fight.

This will serve as your new found knowledge whether you get it from me or another instructor who can supply you with truthful information.

How does this balance against you existing knowledge?

Do nothing at all

This is an option that I know many women have considered.

Should you let the rape or attack go ahead?

Should you let him have his power and control?

Maybe the attacker will go away 'peacefully' if you don't struggle?

If he hits you until he uses up his anger maybe the attack will be over more quickly and the damage will be limited?

Perhaps, if the dispute is domestic, he won't hit you again because he 'loves' you? (not).

This is a difficult area for me to advise you about because it is so personal to you. No two people or situation will be identical.

However, you should consider the following:-

Rape is no longer a physical attack that will be over in a few minutes. It may no longer be a question of getting over the physical damage in a few weeks and being left with the emotional distress. Rape could mean **HIV/AIDS, HEPATITIS B, and DEATH**.

You must ask yourself the question, in this light, **can doing nothing ever be better than doing something?** It is a personal matter only you can finally decide.

As a young, bullied child, I chose to do nothing because I had no other option. But now as an adult I have learnt both practical and theoretical skills that give me many different choices of how I may deal with a problem. But which choice is going to be correct?.

This is the question you will have to think deeply about.

Confronted by many antagonists nightly, I can try out anything from Plato (Greek philosopher) to Punching. You don't have my options.

Your confrontation may never happen, or may be 15 years away, who knows.?

What would you choose to do right now in a rape attempt ?

"Convicted Sex attacker William Stevenson had previous convictions for attacks on women, including one in which he half strangled a victim. He received life for raping a student who he ordered to commit a variety of sex acts, punched her in the face then raped her, while on bail for another attack. After the attack he awarded her six out of 10. The victim told the court "If I had fought him he would only have been more violent so I was submissive,"

133

Identifying an attacker

All forms of crime and physical assault involve a person or persons. So, at some stage, you will need to remember how somebody looks so that others can identify them.
The police use a computerised electronic facial system known as E-FIT which provides expert support to investigating officers by producing an E-FIT image of the suspect's likeness. However, this system is not something that we the general public have access to until a crime has happened and we are asked for an impression of the suspect.

There are many occasions when it would be of value to record someone's likeness for future reference, but we cannot use the sophisticated methods available to the police. Maybe someone is acting suspiciously outside our house or a stranger makes mild threats. In themselves these action's are nothing too serious, but the appearance of the person is worth remembering in case the situation develops.

I would like to present some idea's that I teach in my School girl Self Protection classes in the hope that one of the methods may be of use to you. I don't see why there should only be one method of recognising a face, especially as for most of us, the whole exercise of describing somebody else's facial characteristics is a difficult business.

I teach three different methods of remembering appearances and I always advise my students to mix and match the techniques to suit their own preferences. Finally, all that really matters is that you will be able to describe somebody else's appearance, so that another person can identify them, either to apprehend or to avoid them.

1. DISTINGUISHING FEATURES.

Forget all the basics like blond hair, blue eyes etc. because features such as these are shared by thousands of people. Go straight for the features that are not so common, the **distinguishing features**.
Such features may include tattoos, scars, missing teeth, pierced noses, twitches, anything that is unusual. Most of us have something that is uncommon. My broken nose makes me sniff a lot, very annoying for those around me.
Once these unusual features are listed the common characteristics can be added to flesh out the picture e.g. black hair, brown eyes medium height and so on.

If you think about it, those distinguishing features throw themselves at us whenever we meet people without us having to search for them.
It is impossible not to notice Mr Smith's twitching left eye or the wart on Mr Brown's left cheek.
Just take a look into any school playground and you will hear a host of cruel comments that home in and exaggerate those unusual characteristics of the children. In adult circles too, many nicknames represent pronounced features or peculiarities evident to others, without our knowledge.

2. CARICATURES.

This is where an artist draws a likeness of you in cartoon format but over exaggerates your most pronounced features to make the picture instantly recognisable. The pictures are not intended, generally, to be offensive but they do exaggerate features beyond the natural.
If you are not aware of your own prominent features go and spend a few quid on having such a picture composed.
You may be very surprised how the image you see in the picture varies with what you think you look like. Things get worse if others recognise the likeness immediately.
Caricatures can destroy the ego.

I can remember having my first caricature done down the West End of London while out with some friends. I expected the broken nose, scars and bumps on my forehead but I was also treated a receding hairline and a collection of double chins that had crept up on me over the years.

So, have a look at the people around you and see if you can pull out their prominent features and transfer this into a cartoon of them. You can also include the distinguishing features method to get a good result.

Practice by taking a few glances at a complete stranger and then try to catch them in a caricature drawing. If you practice too often with friends and they get to see the results, you may lose those friends at an alarming rate!! So tread carefully.

3. LOOKALIKES.

This method is quite easy.

You can take almost any individual and find a similarity between them and another person known to you.
That person may be a celebrity, someone from History, a friend, neighbour or member of your family. Infamous people can count just as well as school teachers or mates at work. Anyone living or dead whose likeness is known to you will do.
The similarity needn't cover just appearance for you may notice that the person you are trying to describe holds a cigarette like your uncle Bert or brushes his hair back like Adolf Hitler used to do.

Any connection, no matter how slight may be the one thing that allows others to recognise the same person.
As strange as it may seem some people have even been known to resemble animals e.g. a Boxer dog's face like Winston Churchill, eyes like an owl, or the cruel extreme of the Elephant Man John Merrick.

So, the traditional photo-fit method used by the police is not the only method and maybe, in your case, not the best solution to providing a likeness of someone you need others to recognise.

Emotional cruelty and blackmail

Self protection should aim to go much further than just providing physical techniques, as I've said again and again. It should mean protecting against any form of harm, as opposed to Self Defence, which relates to defence against physical attack only.

Being blackmailed or emotionally harmed are other types of attack that can be used against you and are no less damaging than physical assaults. Sometimes it is all too easy to fall innocently into the trap of emotional cruelty. The results can totally destroy peoples lives and in some cases has led to suicides.
The original act is usually something that you would wish to keep a secret and that others would consider to be wrong or immoral and the revelation would cause deep hurt and embarrassment.
This kind of cruelty can often be seen in children as one child tries to manipulate or control another.

How often have you heard one child saying to another,
"If you don't give me a sweet I'm telling".
This goes on into the teenage and adult years and can become a cruel and emotionally violent means of extorting money, goods or favours from another person.

Blackmail is an arrestable offence of which the Law states the following:-

' A person guilty is guilty of blackmail if, with a view to gain for himself or another or with intent to cause loss to another, he makes any unwarranted demand with menaces; and for this purpose a demand with menaces is unwarranted unless the person making it does so in the belief that he has reasonable grounds for making the demand and that the use of the menaces is a proper means of reinforcing the demand'.

The Law is there to protect you if you are a victim of blackmail so I am not going to cover this area. Instead, I am going to deal with the **emotional cruelty** that has the single intention of causing you the maximum distress possible with no other objective. The effects could cause you embarrassment, shame and emotional pain possibly leaving you utterly discredited.

Teenage boys have often used this type of cruelty, after dating a girl, by spreading rumours such as **'I've had her. She's a slag. She was easy!'**.
Adulthood can change things because women are more able to deal with rumour spreaders, without fearing the repercussions from parents that teenagers dread.
However, adult emotional cruelty can be much worse, as there are more areas vulnerable to attack.

I think the most damaging kind of emotional cruelty suffered by adults is when an initial act is done in all innocence without any fear of reprisals, until another person decides you are no longer flavour of the month and you become a target for them. At this moment that innocent act becomes a weapon to be used against you.

There are many different ways in which emotional harm can be caused to you, such as in stalking, so I will narrow it down to just the few that I feel are pretty much avoidable, which I know have actually happened. My reason for using the examples is to help you avoid similar traps.

The spoken word is over and gone as soon as it is heard and will only be repeated if you choose to repeat it. However, if you record something, be it on audio cassette tape, video tape, photograph, writable CD etc. it is there to seen or heard again and again by anyone.

I have been given consent to use the following examples:-

1. *As a bit of fun a woman gave her husband some photographs of herself, posing topless. She gave the photos to him as she had noticed that he was forever looking at the topless models in newspapers and she was having a gentle dig at him.*

Two years later the couple were going through divorce proceedings. In the course of fighting for their home the husband produced the same photos in an attempt to discredit his wife. He claimed that he had found the photos in the jacket of a male visitor to their house and that as a result he had realised that his wife was having an affair.
The court accepted this untrue version of events and as a result, the woman lost her home, family, and circle of friends and nearly lost contact with her children. The whole case took a downturn because of some photos that were originally intended as nothing more than a light hearted joke.

2. *A married couple used a camcorder to make a home movie of their lovemaking as a way of bonding their marriage. Unfortunately, a year later, the wife had an affair and set up home with her new lover. The wife had forgotten about the video tape but the husband had not.*

The husband later, allegedly, made copies of the tape, had digitised pictures taken from it using a home computer and also had movie animation clips transferred to floppy disc and recordable CD disk.
He was like a time bomb waiting to explode. He claimed that if he was ever denied access to his children, or if they were ever drawn away from him as their father, he would do the following :-

Firstly , he would send the digitised pictures and the animated movie clips out over as many computer networks as he could get access to on the Internet. Anyone with a computer and access to the network would be able to see the photographs and animation free of charge.

Secondly, the photographs would be faxed to anyone to his ex-wife or her new partner's work place or social circle.

Thirdly, he would place an advertisement in her local newspaper offering copies of the Adult home video free of charge.

Finally, he also threatened to use a video sender to send the video directly onto the T.V. screens inside the couple's home and also onto the screens of the night club that the couple visited, using a video sender.

Now, maybe this guy is off his nut acting in this extreme way, but you should now be able to see how much damage can be done with a twenty minute video tape. Do not fall into the same trap because all the above are possible.

3. A husband felt that his marriage was being badly affected by the emotional distress his wife was suffering as a result of child abuse she had suffered from her brother and because her mother had had an affair that she had witnessed and no one else had suspected. The wife would never disclose this information to anyone else for fear of destroying the family.

The husband tried to persuade his wife to seek help from a professional counsellor but she refused. As a result the husband decided to record the next conversation the couple had in which these matters were discussed without his partner's consent or knowledge so he could take it to a counsellor.

However, before the tape ever got to a counsellor, which the husband had originally intended, the marriage collapsed, the couple became enemies and the secret tape became a weapon.

Ask your self the question what would you do if you were in possession of a tape of another person's secrets and they did you enormous harm?
Would you use the tape to seek revenge?

You should now see just how dangerous using an audio tape, still camera or video camera could be if the recorded information were ever to be used against you, no matter how innocent was the original intention.

My advice is never do anything or say anything that could be turned against you if things were to go wrong in a relationship.

Always ask the question

'If I do this now, could the action ever be used as a weapon against me if another person turned against me?'

Admittedly, it would not be possible to stop someone making a secretive recording but it is possible for you to control what you say to others, this also goes for everything you put into writing in the form of love or hate letters.

You should also remember to take care with drinks or drugs, as their effects could encourage you to say all kinds of things that you would normally keep confidential.

Remember, once something is recorded, it may be around for a long time unless the item and all copies are destroyed.

I certainly tread very carefully when letting people into my private life. I have found out the hard way about abuse of trust, don't let it happen to you.

Alcohol and drugs

The effects of alcohol and drugs on our bodies can range from the pleasurable to the frightening and without doubt will cause dramatic changes to the way we react to others. What is the connection to Self Protection? I believe that there are two significant connections.

Firstly, through understanding the effects of stimulants on our own bodies will show us how easy it is to let our guard down and to do something out of character, maybe causing danger to ourselves in the process.

Secondly, this understanding may forewarn you that someone else is under the influence of alcohol or drugs and give you a clue to the way they may act.
Do not mislead yourself into thinking that because you never dabble with intoxicants or mix with people who do, you will never be threatened by someone who is under the influence. So read on further and learn a little more for you own safety.

ALCOHOL

The effects of alcohol are the most instantly recognisable because they are legal and widely available. They generally effect our co-ordination, our balance goes, our speed and reactions are reduced, our Motor fitness rapidly disappears. Our speech will become slurred and we will become drowsy.
One of the worst effects of alcohol is that it instantly makes us brave, we get 'Dutch Courage'. We will become over confident but will lose our ability to protect ourselves if things go wrong.

Conversely, if we are attacked by a drunk he may be difficult to stop because the alcohol anaesthetises the body to pain and your strikes may do nothing.
Your fingertip strike will be all you have so don't forget to practice.

You may think that the effects of drink are known to all and have no place in this book, but **I have intended this book for girls of secondary school age through to adulthood** and whether you accept the reality of youngsters drinking or not, it happens.

Some Drugs are illegal and are varied in appearance and in there effects on a person. They are also easier to slip into someone's drink or food and have the added effect of getting someone hooked and encouraged to do things that break the boundaries of alcohol.

To save time and space. I will list the drugs and its effects and rely on you to apply this information to yourself and an attacker if either, or both of you were under the influence of such substances.

DOPE:

Cannabis resin, which is also known as Hash, Blow, Draw, comes in compressed greenish or golden-brown blocks.
Cannabis oil, is extracted from the resin of the Cannabis plant.
Marijuana, also known as Grass, Pot, which is made from the leaves and flowers of the dried Cannabis plant. This is herbal cannabis.
There are various other names given to these drugs like Ganja, Skunk, Northern lights, Buds, dope, reefa, puff, blunts, smoke, shit, wacky backy, etc which to all intent and purposes can all be classed as the same thing, just some being stronger than others.

It can be smoked on its own but would be too costly for most people, so the normal procedure is to smoke it with tobacco in a roll up, which is called a Joint or Spliff or with a pipe.
You can smell quite easily when its smoked, it give off a strong sweet smell and its effects normally last for several hours.

Some people eat it by putting it in home made cakes and other make a brew and drink it just like tea. This shows you how easy it would be for someone to give it to you without you knowing.

It normally heightens your appreciation of sound and colour whilst giving the sense of relaxation and well being. It affects concentration, slows your reflexes.

Large amounts can cause minor hallucinations, distort vision, and cause short term memory loss.

Regular use can cause unpleasant feelings such as anxiety, slight panic, and paranoia. Smoking dope and drinking Alcohol will give a feeling of nausea which is why most smokers do not drink yet display the effects of alcohol intake.

Although it is claimed that dope smoking is not addictive like other drugs, I know one individual who cannot face the world and its pressures without having a minimum of one smoke a day.

I have seen him befriend someone who had openly issued a death threat only minutes earlier, putting mine, his and other peoples lives at risk while affected by this drug.

I dread the effects of passive smoking that we will all be subjected to if it ever becomes legal.

AMPHETAMINES

Known as Speed, Whiz, Sulphate, Sulph, Uppers, Purple hearts, Sherbet, Billy. It is a man made powder which can also be in capsule or tablet form, usually white in colour. It can be sniffed, swallowed, or injected.

Its effects are a rush of energy, confidence, lack of appetite. The ability to stay awake is boosted greatly, and it speeds up the breathing and heart rate. Regular use can cause nervousness, anxiety, paranoia, damage to blood vessels, mouth ulcers, weight loss, heart failure, and psychiatric problems.

The effects normally last for around 4 hours and cause the taker to move continuously, and speak almost non stop. They are normally over friendly and will offer to do things for you as someone they care a lot for. They will drink plenty of fluids due to dehydration and a serious level of dryness will occur in the lips, mouth and throat.

Their sexual desire will be heightened along with a raised level of risk taking. This is the most impure drug of the drugs market, usually containing as little as 5% of its purity after being mixed (cut) with other agents, the main ones being sugars/glucose, caffeine, and ephedrine.
I have seen sulphate slipped into someone's drink in a night-club, unknown to them while they went to the toilet and I have had a work colleague mix a similar item it in a meal of mine without me knowing, sending me crazy and paranoid whilst working.

Have you ever gone to the toilet in a club and left your drink behind?

Slimming pills are the same type of thing and are now being banned in this country due to their addictiveness and long term effects.

Cocaine

Also called Charlie, Snow, Coke, Wash, Base, Crack, Rock, C, Dust, Lady Snow.
It is a white powder (**Cocaine**) or small white blocks formed by treating with chemicals forming crystals (**Crack**) and made from the **Cocoa** plant.
It is sniffed or injected as Cocaine, or smoked as Crack.

Its effects are exhilaration, feeling of well being, indifference to pain and fatigue, sensations and illusions of great physical strength and mental capacity, confidence, decreased hunger.

After effects include tiredness and depression and regular use can cause unhappiness, restlessness, sickness, weight loss, a feeling of persecution, paranoia, anxiety, panic and hallucinations.

High doses can cause heart attack or breathing failure. Crack is much more addictive than cocaine and it is said that after only taking it once, you will be addicted. Many Crack users also mix and match with heroin to stabilise their moods.

A Crack or Cocaine user *is a very dangerous person to be around* and will be a nightmare of an attacker to stop.

Stay well away and once again, the eyes are your safest means of escape.

Heroin

Known as H, Skag, Smack, Boy, China white, Henery, Junk, Dragon.

A white powder derived from the Opium Poppy, but normally brownish powder once it hits the streets. It can be injected, smoked, sniffed or inhaled. It gives a feeling of warmth, contentment and euphoria. The mind and body functions remain unimpaired.

Many of the effects of Cocaine apply to Heroin but Heroin is thought to be more addictive and damaging. An overdose can cause coma or death and the withdrawal symptoms are severe.

When smoked, heroin is usually placed on tin foil or a spoon, heated and the fumes inhaled. This is known as chasing the dragon.

The Heroin addict in need of their fix will stop at nothing to get the money to buy the drug.

MDMA

Known as Ecstasy, E's, Adam, Burgers, Dennis the Menace, Brownies, Adam & Eve, Rhubarb & Custard, New Yorkers, XTC, Disco Biscuits, Phase 4, etc.
It comes in the form of Tablets, Capsules, and occasionally powder and is swallowed.

The effects produce a relaxed, happy state with no hallucinations, heightened sensations, full of energy, friendly and uninhibited but not out of control. Regular use causes weight loss, insomnia, paranoia, and moodiness. This drug is mainly used in night-clubs to improve dance experience and to create a feeling of universal love and boundless energy.

It is widely believed by youngsters that there is no real danger from use of this drug. However the dangers hit the headlines in the sad case of Leah Betts who took a single £10 Ecstasy tablet on her 18th Birthday and died after 6 days of falling into a coma, in November 1995 .

You can cause your own death from dehydration and overheating. I have seen youngsters so dehydrated that they have attempted to drink the water out of fire extinguishers, which is not healthy considering the anti freeze agents also inside.
Ecstasy sometimes contains Ketamine which is anaesthetic. If used in high quantities can knock you on the floor leaving you unconscious.

So Self Protect yourself and steer clear from this drug, no matter how fashionable or trendy it is supposed to be.

LSD

Known as Acid, Tabs, Trips, Tripping, Tabs, Blotters, Flash, Lucy, and are taken by mouth.
Comes in various forms such as small white or brown tablets, blotting paper soaked in chemicals, sugar cubes, and small squares of paper showing various patterns or logo's.

Effects include intensified colours, visual or aural distortions, heightened perceptions, hallucinations, depression, dizziness, disorientation, panic, a sense of profundity, acute paranoia, and anxiety.
The day after will give the effect of an hangover and it has been said that you can also suffer from flashbacks years later.

This again is another drug that is more danger to you than anything else. Stories have circulated about people have jumped off buildings thinking they can fly after taking LSD..

"Newsletter - Robert Clack school - Dagenham September 96
Police Alert, drugs, particularly LSD are being pushed locally at children."

ANABOLIC STEROIDS

Common trade names are Durabolin, Stromba, plus dozens more.

This is not the type of drug you will often come across in your travels, but is one that you need to be aware of.

It is taken by tablet, capsule or injection by bodybuilders who want to increase muscle size and strength.
Its long term use causes damage including jaundice, liver tumours, premature heart disease, and increased aggressiveness.

TV documentaries on crime against women have indicated that constant use of Anabolic steroids by male bodybuilders has shown that they create a higher than normal sex drive, combined with a heightened level of aggressiveness.

Interviews were conducted with a group of males who had attacked female's, both sexual and aggressively and it was found that all those interviewed were affected by the taking of Anabolic steroids.

Research is still going on into the study of the effects of Anabolic steroids which will hopefully give more information in this area., but based on the information currently available, I would avoid constant steroid users like the plague.

AMYL & BUTYL NITRATE

Common names are Poppers, Ram, TNT, Rush, Snappers, Nitrates, Bananas.

A clear yellow inflammable liquid which smells sweet when fresh, but like dirty socks when stale. It was originally designed for Angina sufferers in the form of a glass capsule which was popped and inhaled to treat heart pains. If swallowed rather than inhaled, it can cause death.

Its effect are a rushing sensation of loosened sexual and dancing experiences. Headaches, vomiting, dermatitis, reduced blood pressure resulting in unconsciousness or heart attacks.

It is openly sold in most sex shops and is widely available.

Magic Mushrooms

Also known as Liberty Cap, Shrooms, Mushies. These can come fresh or dried and are recognised by their thin stalks and caps the size of a fingernail. The effects are mild hallucinations, feeling relaxed, energetic and elated. Stomach cramps and feeling sick. Being locked in a room with someone suffering the effects of drinking mushroom tea can be a frightening experience.

Solvents

This is commonly known as Glue sniffing or Huffing, and take place by sniffing the fumes of many household products like aerosol's, stain removers, lighter fuel refills, thinners, and solvent based glues. The effects are intoxication, like being drunk on alcohol.

I was witness to a young girl caught in the act of glue sniffing by her mother. The girl was already beyond the world or reality and reasoning. As the mother attempted to coax the girl to hand over the plastic bag filled with glue, the girl grabbed a knife and pushed it to her mothers throat while dishing out verbal abuse. The girl remembered nothing the next day.

Deaths have occurred from users inhaling their own vomit after falling into unconsciousness and also from squirting aerosol gasses directly into their mouths, freezing their air passages.

"A GIRL of 15 was raped by the policeman detailed to take her to hospital after she was found suffering from the effects of solvent abuse. Pc Adam Grice-Roberts, carried out the attack in his patrol car. The girl collapsed in an alley "insensible" from inhaling butane gas to which she is addicted."

Sedatives & Tranquillisers

Alcohol crosses the barrier of similarity with Downers or Depressants because it supplies similar effects and like all other drugs listed below its not illegal if issued and used correctly within the law as prescribed..

Barbiturates are commonly known as Barbs, Downers, Blues, Reds, Sekkies, Sleepers.While Tranquillisers are known as Tranx, Benzos, Eggs, Jellies, Temazepam, Valium, Librium.
Gammahydroxybuttyrate, known as GHB, GBH, and Liquid Ecstasy is a colourless slightly salty liquid.

The user has a feeling of warmth, contentment, relaxation and stress relief, increased sexual drive, loss of co-ordination, sickness, unconsciousness. This is widely used in Gay Clubs and social circles.
It is hard to believe all the different drugs that available out there.

I haven't touched on Smart drugs (Nootropics) or plant drugs (entheogens) that have effects on the body & mind depending on how you use them.

This will fill a book on its own however in brief the smart drugs are used for things like memory improvement and cognitive alertness, whereas the plant drugs are more directed to getting stoned or having hallucinations.

Their availability in the UK would make them harder to find than any of the other drugs listed, with much less an effect, so I do not think they really have place within this self protection book.

Verbal - visual scanning of environment

One of the main reasons we get attacked, is that we are pre-occupied, thinking of something else other than our safety.

Our brain is engaged and leaves no room for thought of the dangers that may be lurking around the corner.

So how do we stop ourselves from letting our mind wander ?

A method used by professional bodyguards, security, doormen, and other similar professionals is verbal - visual scanning of the environment. In plain English this means telling yourself a story which involves you and all that surrounds you, including buildings, walls, hedges, cars, animals, people etc.
By doing this you will be thinking of nothing other than what's going on around you, Your brain will be fully engaged with a second by second account of your life as it is now.

This will automatically **raise your awareness** and enable you to **evaluate possible dangers**, which will aid you in **avoidance of danger**. If you take a closer look at yourself you will see that you may already do this with daily tasks, here in an example.

Your are out shopping, you have the kids with you, you are pushed for time, your budget is limited etc. You are pushing the trolley, scanning the shelves for products, switching over then to the kids to see they are not fighting, wandering off, or being taken away, you then check your watch, you make sure the trolley contents fit in with your budget, you check sell by dates and so on. You go through the scanning routine hundreds of times to ensure that you get away with no problems.

Now just imagine if you were not switched on to what's going on around you and you wandered around the supermarket day dreaming about your 'underwater basket weaving' class at college last week.

Your rain will be fully engaged with trivia connected with this subject and no room is left for, or attention paid to your shopping list, kids, time, budget, safety etc. The shopping trip turns into a nightmare.
The kids knock down the stacked tins, play football with the butter, the basket filled with products that nobody remembered putting in the basket, a child runs off, etc. You end up in a real state, just because you are switched off.

We scan continuously when we drive and continually check our current position so we can avoid danger. I remember when I was training to be a driving instructor. My tutor would suddenly put his hand over the rear view mirror so I could not see behind and ask " What is behind us now? ", or " We just passed a traffic sign, what was it ? ".

These were all methods of checking whether I was visually scanning the things I should be. Sometimes I would just drive and give a verbal report as I'm scanning, to show I was switched on and not mind wandering.

It would go something like this " My speed is 25 MPH, red escort to rear, blue Volvo in front, road sign shows traffic light ahead, dog by tree ahead, red escort overtaking, lowering my speed to 20 MPH, children ahead playing with ball, etc. ".

I had been using this system for years so found it easy.

My introduction to this observation skill actually came around 15 years ago from Geoff Britton, a friend who just happened to be working within the area of Security versus the professional shoplifter.

He showed me how the scanning skills of both the shoplifter and the security staff would work against each other and compete to win the day.

Ironically it was Geoff who also encouraged me to move on in life and teach what I was good at, Self protection, and gave me my first girls school to teach at when he moved to Spain which ultimately brought about the existence of this book.

I had to use my scanning skills big time when I took my kids to Florida's Disneyworld for 2 weeks. I went from seeing them once a week, taking them out for the day to the pictures, park etc. all local to me, to the culture shock of Disney's 43 square miles of everything imaginable that could possibly pre occupy your mind, and thousands of kids around you.

Now add to this the fact that my little girl was 4, and the boys were aged 6, 9, and 14, all having their individual interests drag them in 4 different directions for 12 hours a day for 2 weeks with me solely responsible for their care, safety, and returning them back to England to their mother. Phew!!!

 My visual scanning skills were on overtime, I stayed switched on and scanned like an owl from around 10am to 10pm without slacking.

I am used to visual scanning through my work on the door and get to practice it for around 7 hours each night and I consider myself to be pretty good at it. This skill can be worked on and perfected.

The hardest thing to do is to stop yourself becoming pre-occupied (daydreaming) with crap. As soon as you engage your brain with useless thought, you have lost sight of your surroundings, changed situations, and are at risk.

Even while working I will not let anyone engage my brain with trivia, I just continue to scan and scan and let them waffle on.
Now think about how little thought you give to checking out your environment when out travelling from A to B.

You will see that all you thoughts are concerned with what you are going to do when you reach your Destination, or other matters. But not your second by second scanning for your own personal safety.

Try this next time you go out along a route that you have travelled many times before.
Talk to yourself in your thoughts (Not verbally for fear of getting locked up) and tell yourself everything you see including, Animals, People, Vehicles and their position, Change of Direction, threat to your personal space, Dark and unlit areas, Doorways, alleys, Bushes, fences, and so on. Don't forget to check out windows of houses to see who could be watching you, as you pass by.

I have spent so much time on scanning my own environment, which becomes second nature if you have been involved in real heavyweight life threatening situations, that I cannot switch off in daily life.
I can never fully lock into a tunnel vision eye contact conversation with one person. I automatically scan and constantly find and update myself on what's going on around me. It almost makes me appear rude and uninterested in the person I am talking to, but those that know me well, understand why I am like this.

I have perfected my scanning to such a degree that It is almost an impossibility to engage my brain with trivia, or get more than a one line answer from me when I am working.

Practice your scanning, build up on it until you are able to visually scan for the possibility of where dangers could exist. Eliminate the possibility of an ambush or surprise attack.

It will take some work but its worth it.
I can remember once at work when I could see an ambush situation developing. I watched it build up over an hour with each new addition to the group plotting up one by one.

I even knew which person held the knife which was intended for me. The other guys who were working with me saw nothing, they were not switched on, were not scanning.

They just considered it normal that a group of men were standing outside our club at 1am staring at us. Everything else around us was closed. Considering two of them had made a death threat earlier in the evening and said they will be back for us when the club ends. I think that my assessment was the correct one while the others said I was being paranoid.
A bit like saying Salman Rushdie was being a little paranoid.

Learn from this.....
You only have one life to protect, if you make a wrong assessment, you may lose it.

I trusted my visual scanning ability more than I trusted their engaged brains exchanging trivia with each other. You must do the same.
Scan your environment and act upon what you see. Believe me, you will see things in life that you never knew existed, you will become a very hard person to launch a surprise attack on.

Bruce Lee was famous for the teacher student clip in Enter the dragon when he pointed at the sky and asked a student what he saw. The student focused on the finger and was slapped for missing the heavenly glory. The lesson here was that if you focus on one thing alone you will miss what's really going on.

What you looking at ?

The classic one liner that stops you in your tracks. But what is the big deal with this phrase?. Well it's not the wording that confuses us, *it's the confusion that's going on inside our heads that we find hard to deal with*. Combine this with the adrenal rush and you have a situation where you have lost the fight before it begins.

We all tend to concentrate on trying to answer the question but never find a suitable response *and still miss the point*.

Let's face it !they know exactly who your looking at , even if as in most cases it's a mere accidental glance. So what's really going on?

1. you are thinking about nothing in particular
2. you are suddenly confronted with **"what are you looking at"** ?.
3. *now you are thinking plenty like, what do I do? did I look ? are they going to hit me ?*
4. the brain senses danger and you get the adrenal rush, the shakes etc.
5. *you get hit.*

The whole problem lies in number 3 *now you are thinking plenty*

It is at this point that **your brain becomes engaged**.

Don't try to find the answer.

As from now , prepare your response. Prepare your response so that it's ready for when this or a similar quote is thrown at you in order to engage your brain and mess up your thought pattern which will set off your panic alarms.

Forget about the school playground responses such as such as
" I don't know it's not labelled" etc.
Get in the real world.

If I walked up to you in the street and you didn't know me, I could practically make you piss your pants with a threatening look and a few words. I've had to do it many times in order to survive in my line of work so imagine if an aggressor decided to do it to you for real ?
The next question now is how you are going to respond ?

To test yourself get a friend to front you with the phrase, without preparing for it. Just respond as you would. Then plan a response and try it that way. I can' t decide for you what your response should be, but here are some points to think about.

Whether you respond physically or verbally, is it going to be ?

Passive = sorry I caused offence I thought you was an old school friend
aggressive = you, Arsehole, what of it.
Silence = your brain will begin thinking, it's engaged.

Preemptive strike = you feared for your safety and hit out
Crazy = act or say something that gives the impression of being Psychopathic it frightens most people shitless, even the toughest aggressor may fear the unknown.
Another point to consider is to capture yourself on video responding in different way's until you see a side of you that you wouldn't like to mess with, or come up against in the street.

159

I had a student who needed to work on a suitable response that would stop an aggressor going any further than a verbal attack. He was having real problems with it.

I was playing the role of an aggressor and from my angle, this student wouldn't have frightened a flee. The only way I could get the student to realise how weak his response was when confronted, was to make a videotape of him, then let him look at himself on TV.

This student realised that this verbal response was to much of a mouthful to get out in a panic situation. There were to many word's, so he had to cut it down to three or four word's. He also realised that he smiles when responding or trying to be aggressive which, was a nervous facial reaction.

No matter how much time we spent on this and how much we tried to rid of the smile it was always there. Its not easy getting a nice natured guy to be nasty.

In the end we decided to **work with the smile rather than try to erase it** (*If you can't beat them - join them*). We studied the psychotic smile that Jack Nicholas used in the 1980 film **The Shining** and combined it with some of prince Naseem Hamed **"Do I look scared ?** (smile) " when he won his World Boxing title and found that we had cracked it.

He had something finally that worked for him which fell in to the category of being crazy.

I can remember a situation that happened to me a few years back when I was confronted in a lift in Covent garden with about eight other people present. None were known to me.

A tall aggressive giant of a man stepped in and for some reason took a dislike to me, I could feel his stare cutting through me like a lazer beam. The lift doors closed and I knew it was going to hit me with *" what you looking at "*. I wasn't far wrong.

For some unknown reason a Clint Eastwood side of me came out. I replied *" Try your luck "*. It was not planned, it was just a phrase that I and all my friend's used at that time in my life. It was just the comical sort of thing's that we would try on each other, joking about. We would say to each other *" Go on then, try your luck "* whether it be with a pretty girl, a fight, a bet, whatever, and that's the first thing that come out of my mouth. I had just managed to get the word's out before the adrenal rush put me into hi pitch mode.

Bingo it worked, He came back with *" Best we forget about it then "*. I was well relieved. I would have had my hand's full with this loony and would only have fought him if he forced me to. So work on your response and have it ready because the phrase *" what you looking at ? "*, is an entry technique, that the aggressor's will always use, will always be there, and will never go away. However it is not the only one you will get confronted with so work on your responses so that you have one that will work for you.

Mapping out your route home

If you look at any journey that any person makes, you will be able to tear it to pieces as far as **areas of danger** are concerned. We will always find that dark alley, that ride in a lift, that dodgy area that we drive through, and so on. We can never eradicate every possibility of danger happening, but we can reduce it dramatically whether it be via foot or transport..

Driving from A to B.

Make sure your fuel is sufficient to enable your journey without having to stop at a garage for a refill. It has not been unknown for someone to jump in the back seat of a car whilst the driver has gone to pay. Also many cars have been stolen from garages because they have been re-fuelled and are warmed up, some with the baby strapped into the seat.

Try to tell someone the route you are going to take, departure and arrival time.

Avoid getting caught at red traffic lights by altering your speed on their approach. If you think about how many times you have been caught by the windscreen washing gangs at lights, this will give you an idea as to the possibility of being attacked or forced to drive elsewhere by an attacker. It takes only seconds.

Don't let yourself get flagged down by a confidence trick, a calculated plan of attack. What seems to be an emergency, can destroy all safety plans and logical thought in seconds. If possible carry a mobile phone and make sure that the battery is sufficiently charged up for the journey.

Use your Visual scanning of the environment and if you really want to you can travel whilst speaking your journey into a Dictaphone. Its a good way of recording strange looking peoples features at certain landmarks at certain times, or even car registrations, details of a car and how many people are in that car. It may sound a little extreme but it works.

I first came across this idea when I was learning new journeys for a project I was working on. My memory for roads & places was terrible, so I would speak the journey into my Dictaphone as I was driving. I could then write out my route when I returned home and Balance this out with a map and advice from others to fine tune my journey.

It was then that I discovered how easy it was to record the details of the lunatics that threaten our safety and our lives on today's roads. I think that modern vehicles should all have Dictaphone facility build into our dashboards.

Keep all your doors and windows locked from the inside whilst driving. I know some people say that they would not lock their doors through fear of having an accident and being locked in a car where outside helpers would not be able to get the door open. Its for you to decide which or the two choices pose the biggest threat to you on the journey that you are going to take.

Road Rage

Road rage is nothing new. The media have just found a new name for this phenomenon that has captured the publics imagination. Yet go back as far as you, like even to the old silent movies and you will see road rage. Vehicles were always used to deal with and create car related problems.

What we need to look at is why road rage becoming the problem of violence that it is.

I have come to the conclusion that the protective metal shell of the car has a psychological effect on our minds by giving us a suit of armour with the added benefit of also giving us the power and control to back off or make a charge like a knight in shining armour.

It allows us to shout, swear, become outraged, curse, make offensive gestures, and threaten other drivers, whilst knowing we can hide behind our protective shell and drive away if we need to.
We would not act the same way to those self same individuals if passing them in the street, because we know it would probably end up in a fight and we may get hurt.

Our protective shell is not there, we think more wisely before acting stupidly.

Granted, naturally aggressive people are going to kick off whether they are in a car or not.

"Stephen Cameron, 21, was stabbed to death on a motorway slip road at Swanley, Kent in front of his fiancee in May 96 after a road rage incident."

The protective feeling of the car shell only gives psychological protection through security and equality to those that would not normally confront others in a one to one confrontation in the street.

"A woman was seriously injured in a road rage attack which killed her friend Wayne Margrave. Paul Conlon killed Mr. Margrave as he lay injured in the road from an earlier hit and run accident which had left his leg broken..
Miss Woolford suffered a broken collar bone as she was dragged along the road by Conlon's car as he drove straight at her and Mr Margrave in January 95. Mr Margrave was crushed to death by Mr Conlon's car. The whole incident was brought on because Mr.Conlon was angered at the crowd obstructing the path he wanted to take in his car"

As road rage in my opinion is a psychological problem, I think that it is best dealt with a psychological response.

If you make a mistake, acknowledge your error by waving and apologising. If you feel another driver is giving you a hard time, avoid eye contact and drive as smoothly and calmly as possible. They may see any sudden accelerating or braking as a challenge which is something you want to avoid.

Much that I have already covered applies to this form of threat. Mapping out your route home, having a mobile phone to hand, a Dictaphone to record an attackers appearance or vehicle details, methods of remembering attackers features, keeping your car locked whilst driving, and other such forms of awareness-evaluation and avoidance of confrontation, and always think if a situation is simple, serious or life threatening.

No matter how badly or aggressively another motorists driving may be, never retaliate by racing them or cutting them up. Also do not swear at them or make gestures to intimidate or insult them. Road rage attackers are often looking for an excuse to vent their anger so avoid confrontation.

Recent cases have led to serious injuries and even death. Is it really worth it?

"Paul Erkiert, 41 was jailed for six months after pleading guilty to assaulting a woman by punching her in the face and assaulting her 15-year-old daughter. He had a string of convictions for violence or aggression against women drivers"

Let them think they have won the confrontation making them happy as you would with the domestic abuse situation. Its you who has really won.

Other tips to bear in mind are:-

Keep your distance from the vehicle in front, allowing plenty of space for your sharp exit if threatened seriously from the front or the rear.

Try to keep a space between your car and any parked cars, or other obstacles on your nearside. This will ensure that you will not get boxed in if you have to stop your car, leaving you room to escape if another driver traps you in via your off side.

If you are faced with another driver intent on causing road rage, try to drive towards a police station, fire station, hospital etc where you will be able to draw plenty of attention towards yourself and get immediate help.

Finally, if you are threatened by another motorist, to the point where you fear for your own safety, stray in the car. If you can, phone the police, switch on your hazard lights and sound your horn, attracting as much attention as possible.

Mini cabs, Taxi cabs, or accepting lifts home

I feel the safest form is by our Traditional licensed Black Cabs but problems have still been known to arise.

If you have a Taxi cab taking you to a destination, phone your destination and speak to someone giving departure and expected arrival time, and most important of all the license plate registration, along with the number of the cab's license plate displayed on the square plate fixed to the boot of the car. You can also include a brief description of the driver if you want. It will make no difference to the cab driver if he has to wait for you to make a call because his meter will be running. If you live alone you can leave these details on your own answer-phone. It helps if something goes wrong.

Mini cabs

" Mini cab driver Tariq Moohammed was jailed for five and a half years for raping his passenger after dropping off her friend. The cab company was regularly used and trusted by her parents "

I just don't like mini cabs, full stop. Maybe because most of my mates have cabbed at some time and all of them were ducking and diving in some way, or were hiding from the Dss, had no insurance, and even one who had no licence because he was banned. There was enough criminal records between the lot of them to form a record collection.

I agree, this shows mini cabs in a bad light when there are many respectable, law abiding, professional mini cab drivers out there, but its your safety I am concerned with here, which far outweighs any offence I may cause.

Working in London I see the streets full of pirate mini cab drivers who tout for business with no one other than themselves knowing where they are from.

Some areas are now licensing their mini cab drivers like they do their doormen in an attempt to dispose of the bad element. However, being licensed does not prove you are not a bad person, It just proves that you have done a course, paid a fee, and your details are held by the local authority and the police. This does not stop fake badges being made up as has been done many a time.

If you have to order a mini cab, try to order it from a company local to your home. Use all the same measures that you would use with a Taxi cab, and also get the registration and the car details of the mini cab that is going to pick you up.

Many a time Ive seen girls exit a night club expecting a cab from x Company, only to have jumped into a tout's cab claiming he has been sent. I knew they were touts because they would hang around the night clubs every night looking for business. Little did they know that I had their details at hand should anything ugly happen to a passenger.

Pornography is a man's world

The world of porn is created mainly by men, __using women, to entertain men.__
Looking at it from this perspective. It creates employment and provides entertainment but what about the hidden effects of this world of entertainment and employment ?

Does Porn satisfy a sexual need or does it begin an uncontrollable urge to find sexual satisfaction at any cost _regardless of the consequences_ ?

This book is hoping to make you see the darker side of life so as to enable you to avoid being abused. Let's take a trip down the route.
There is no doubt that a sexual empire has been set-up for men that would not exist if there was not a market for it.
You can find sex in the top shelf girlie magazines, shops specialising in pornographic films - magazines - and love toys, satellite channels devoted to soft and hard porn, calendars displaying topless & nude models, internet sites serving whatever you ask for, daily papers with topless model's, computer images of sex & porn, prostitutes in the streets - visiting homes - or working from brothels, sex phone lines to listen to sexy talk or live girls talk sexy to you, peep shows, strip clubs, topless barmaids, and even private sex parties advertised in most local papers - only obvious to those who know what to look for.

I bet you did not realise there was so much out there related to sex to entertain men ?

The most sickening thing about it all is that with all these forms of sexual gratification available for men - __WOMEN STILL GET RAPED !__

So does this mean that with all these routes of satisfaction available, there still lies this desire to have something that is a challenge rather than an offer ?

I think that every right minded male can be satisfied with which ever of the routes of sexual satisfaction that they choose to follow. However the sick monster who chooses the route of raping for satisfaction, cannot be satisfied by anything other than forcing rape, humiliation, and torture on a victim against their will. It is not really about sexual gratification, its about **Power and Control.**

Of all the sexual resources available to man, their is nothing available to substitute the desire of a rapist wanting to rape, nothing can replace his desire for Power and control over his victim..

Around 10 years ago I opened up a full time Self Defence Gymnasium in London. I rented the building off a Massage Parlour who operated with a few "Working girls" who often had problems with customers, who knew that the girls would never involve the police, for obvious reasons.

I ended up teaching the girls self protection in exchange for information that I wanted on men and why they go to prostitutes. I wanted as much information as I could for a Female Self Protection book I was going to write. After a period of time and study, it was quite clear that men would visit the girls to get some form of sexual satisfaction that they could not, or would not ask their partner for, or they were unable to find a partner for various reasons.
E.g. Not many females would be into their partner dressing up in a nappy & crawling around the floor like a baby, before being breast fed etc. Hence the visit to the working girls.

Some just wanted to be with a female after losing their wives through bereavement or divorce. And others found it more economical to spend £x with a guarantee of being satisfied rather than spending the same on taking a female out and possibly getting nothing.

I spoke to over 20 working girls about rapist's and how sexual satisfaction may be used to kill the desire to rape. I thought that I may discover something that would stop the rapist and make my book a best seller.

I concluded quite clearly that **NOTHING WILL STOP THE RAPIST**. Rapist's do not visit working girls, *because they cannot be satisfied in this way. There would be an element missing*. They would get the sex that they wanted, when they wanted, but would not get the buzz from torture, pain and humiliation that they would get from an unwilling victim. They would **not get genuine power and control**.

How could any prostitute convince a rapist that the attack is genuine ? Nothing could fill the gap of the real fear and terror that they inflict on the victim.

I came to the conclusion that none of the sexual satisfaction resources available turned anyone into a rapist, as none of them would satisfy or deter a rapist.

The rapist was in a category all of his own that could only be dealt with in one way. Avoidance and punishment. You are going to have to avoid an encounter with a rapist
FOR THE REST OF YOUR LIFE.

If you are unfortunate enough to get attacked then the next step is their punishment, whether it be from you, the Law, or both.

Knives & other edged weapon's

If it can cut its an Edged weapon. Don't focus on it for a short moment and forget about it, or ignore its threat. Knives are always a threat as edged weapons, and are normally the only weapon that draws our attention.

The next in line is the broken bottle or beer glass which is evident in our pubs and night-clubs and these also are classed as edged weapons.
There are many other items that are used to cut and maim, but do not seem evident because we recognise their existence for some task **other than for harming people**.

Consider the case of football thugs that toured the towns and cities of the opposing team's and left little traps, messages of hate for people who were guilty of nothing more than living in an area where the match was played. It mattered not whether they actually supported their local football team.

The thugs would leave double edged razor blades imbedded in bars of soap in the toilets of trains, train station's, football grounds, pubs, restaurant's, etc, with the sole aim of cutting the opposing team's supporters to shreds as they washed their hands, oblivious to the fact that the hidden razor was slicing them.

How about the demented thugs who fixed razors to the sliding surface of children's slides in local parks. This sickening act took place only a few years ago. These are all horrific crimes perpetrated by those that have no care for the harm that an edged weapon will cause. So, if this is the case, **do you think these same monsters will think twice about stabbing or cutting you ?**

"19 year old Katrina Taylor was stabbed 6 times in the chest. Her body was found dumped in a graveyard in Brighton"

I am not concerned here with the trained knife fighter, because your chance of meeting one of these and being challenged to a fight is as likely as winning the lottery.

Even if you were so unlucky, as we all think we are, they would cut you to shreds in seconds. So that is not a worry, and to be honest, anyone that I have ever come across that was trained with a knife, are far removed from the scum bags that are likely to threaten your life for the contents of a purse.

Also when I say trained with a knife, I am referring to those that study the Filipino stick and edged weapon arts like Master Danny Guba & Val Pableo pictured below. Also others Specialised in military weapon training, and likewise.

I am not talking about weapon wielding idiots who have read a martial art or military book and have subscribed to a home study course including free knife.

173

Now I have made it clear as to which group I am excluding and my reasons for doing so, I will now address were the threat lies.

"Geoffrey Adams was jailed for life after he stabbed and seriously injured an elderly woman and wounded two police officers. she lost an eye in the attack as he was slashing her face and head."

"15-year-old Naomi Smith was sexually assaulted and stabbed to death after she went out to post a letter. Her body was found under a slide in a playground."

"Donna Mead, 25, her throat cut and was stabbed repeatedly in the at the home of ex-boyfriend."

"90-year-old Annie Saxton was stripped naked, sexually assaulted, stabbed, battered and throttled to death in her home in a sheltered housing complex. Some of her injuries were inflicted after death."

"Babysitter Rachel Rooney, 15, and seven year old Jonathan Copley were stabbed to death and their throats cut in the boy's bedroom."

"Stephen Wilkinson killed schoolgirl Nikki Conroy. He stabbed her 10 times with such ferocity that the blade passed through her body three times. He also wounded two other girls at Hall Garth school when he barricaded the door, made the children kneel down with their eyes closed, and began stabbing them."

"Natalie McLean, 18, was found a week after being stabbed to death in her flat. She had been half-eaten by her starving pet puppy. A stab wound in the neck was the most likely cause of death but was hard to determine because of the amount of flesh missing from the body."

"Vivian Hutchinson, 26, was stabbed to death on her doorstep in front of her daughter and niece after she had answered the door of her house at about 11pm to a group of young males."

"Stuart Williamson, who was released from jail after killing his girlfriend four years ago, stabbed his mother Audrey Fisher to death with a kitchen knife as she was having a new alarm system installed to protect herself from him"

Always remember though! these are just *my opinions*. So read through and consider the alternatives to my theory of edged weapons, and decide for yourself what you think is best for you in order to recognise and survive an edged weapon attack. AN estimated 14,000 flick knives, cut-throat razors, swords and bayonets had been handed in to 3,000 bins located at police stations across England and Wales in over a four-week knife amnesty. The amnesty was established after a London headmaster, Philip Lawrence, a 48-year-old father-of-four, was fatally stabbed in December 95.

At the time of writing I worked in an environment where 80% of the customers were born and bred in a knife carrying culture as a way of life, and range from those that have trained naturally with knives as we do in football or netball, hockey, to those that have become good to very professional.

In short, almost everyone in my work environment has studied knife at some point, so I have watched, listened, and have also fought when I've had to. I have also spent hundreds of hours training and exploring the lethal street application of knives.

This is what tells me that the truly skilled knife fighter is not your concern.

I still have all my limbs through being skilful and switched on, and luckily not meeting the professional of the edged weapon culture. If I was to, I have no doubt that I would have more stripes than a zebra, unless I was able to balance the scales a little, like having a machine gun and a 50 foot gap between us. So lets move on and focus on the real threat....

Anything that can cut, tear, or plunge into you is an edged weapon, whether or not it was designed for this purpose.

My eyesight was saved by the bone of my forearm when an edged weapon was slashed across my face. The scar on my arm serves as a constant reminder.

My lung was saved by my lower rib when I was sliced in the gut. My forehead was split open on two occasions by different edged weapons. The crack across my crown was made with a ball and chain style edged weapon.

All incidents were unrelated and happened over the years for various reasons that do not matter here. All that matters is the fact that they were all done with the tip of an edged weapon by someone who wanted to cut, pierce or open up part of my body by people who were not trained in weapon fighting.

I have just been unlucky in some ways but also lucky in that I survived.

We face the danger of an edged weapon everytime we open up a can of food and we use our own edged weapons everyday to bite and chew our food (our teeth).

Recognising edged weapons is one thing, but how do we deal with them?

What do you do to stop that screwdriver being plunged into our chest, that crushed drinks can from tearing our face flesh apart, that snapped phone card from slicing open our Carotid artery?

Basically its down to schools of thought and their opinions, leaving you to decide what you think will work best for you.

All you can do is input all the information you can relating to edged weapons, play devils advocate with it and hopefully you will be able to make an informed choice as to which options are suited to you..

You must remember though that I am not going to give you martial arts movements to practice as the answer to an edged weapon. That's of no use to an untrained person.

Rather, I am going to supply theoretical information that may be the deciding factor for your survival.

As far back as you go in time you will find edged weapons designed to slash, stab & kill. An edged weapon is silent and never needs reloading. Frightening isn't it.

So how are you going to deal with it?

No material possessions can be worth testing your luck with a knife, so if an attacker is only after your money or possession's, hand them over.
Also if you get the opportunity and you think its safe to do so, throw the items they want into the opposite direction that you want to exit from. Let them gather the goods while you run & scream until you know its safe to stop and commend yourself for saving your life.
The real problem only exists when the weapons becomes a tool of the trade for the rapist.
Do you hand over your body as you would your possessions ?
Lets take a realistic look at the options.

To help you to think clearly, I ask you now to **forget about yourself and remove yourself from the equation**!

Apart from our younger readers of this book, Sex is something that we all do or have done some time in our life. However the way that society has developed its outlook on different types and methods of obtaining sexual satisfaction, we are looked upon by our peers with scrutiny according to what they see as acceptable.

This creates a problem with our thinking and reduces our option's.

Eg.

A group of lads having a drink get onto the topic of male raping male using a knife as a weapon!

Peer pressure instantly takes away any option or choice of how the male will deal with the confrontation. Even faced with the fact that he may lose his life, he will never consider submitting to the rapist. He will kill the rapist or die trying..

Well that's the story he tells the lads, that's the story they want to hear, everyone is happy and macho and have another pint..

Peer pressure alters our logical thinking when we think of ourselves as the victim. Now if any of these guys took themselves out of the picture and discussed the same problem using their own son as the victim, options would begin to pop up all over the place, and believe me the option of their son sacrificing their life would not exist!

Its time for "stuffing peer pressure, and thinking logically".

When I was married, the subject of females being raped was discussed. I asked my ex wife

" what would you do if you were raped?"

She said that she wouldn't be able to tell me because I would say things like- she asked for it, she could have avoided it, I would disown her, I would track down and kill the rapist, and so on...

Now even as a self protection instructor, I was not listening to any of these words. All I was waiting to hear was **" I would kill anybody that tried to touch me "**.

178

That was my form of comfort which I needed at the time to convince myself that nobody was going to touch my wife.

I needed to hear her say such words before I could drop the subject. I would never even consider the fact that she may think its better to go through the rape ordeal rather that have the children visit her grave.

Thankfully this never happened and was only a conversation, but can you see how powerful peer pressure can be. I pressured her into giving a reply that would make me happy and refused to accept any alternative.. Sad but true....

I hope I am putting my point across loud and clear. Peer pressure exist and denies us the option of choice when we include ourselves as the possible victim.

So if you want to look at the edged weapon threat clearly, you will have to apply all your values and decisions on a life other than yours, **a life that is priceless to you.**

Consider the victim being your daughter, sister, mother, etc. Will you advise them to fight to the death if confronted with a rapist using a knife?

Or will you say "stuff peer pressure" and find another way to survive? **It changes your thinking doesn't it.**

Here are some safety tips.....

Always try to keep or create a reactionary gap between you and the attacker, you life may depend on time and distance so use it wisely. I know it all sounds easier than it will be but I only have the option of giving you some advice, against giving non at all.

Creating distance is important. If I can cover 15 feet within 2 seconds, I'm sure some crazed hard-on loony can do the same, so create as much distance as possible.

Think of anything to stall for time. If rushed, side step at the very last minute like a bull fighter does then hit the exit.

Take advantage of any thing around you that can be utilised as a weapon. Putting your bag or elbow through a glass window will make a noise and also give you an edged weapon. Be prepared to use maximum force to stop the rapist.

Never lose sight that he may intend to seriously harm, or kill you.
Does he have the ability to get that edged weapon close enough to you to harm you?

If weapon contact is unavoidable, grab the weapon hand and smash it into the wall, floor, or anything that will damage the hand and force them to lose the weapon.
Don't let go of the weapon hand unless you can escape, you may have pissed him off big time by taking away his power and control momentarily, and his instant reaction may kill you.

I'm basing the above options around the fact that you are untrained, and are confronted with a weapon threatening rapist, and the fact that an edged weapon of even less than an inch long, can kill you.

It is for you to decide for yourself what is right for you, I can only advise you of some of the possibilities so you have an informed choice.

To date, the martial art have still not solved the problem of a knife attack (in my opinion) and the law of the land imposes further restrictions on us.

180

So you will have to decide if being law abiding and losing your life, is a better option than chancing prosecution and possible imprisonment in order to survive.

I personally, would have to be killed by any man that attempted to knife rape me. It is the only way he would be able to stop me ripping his eyes out, biting through his carotid artery, ripping his penis from his body, before I really turned nasty.

Nothing to do with my peers. I have the physical ability and a "do or die" mental attitude that will explode if I become faced with becoming a target of a violent sexual attack.

My choice is based on my own personal ability and dislike for perpetrators of sex crimes. Its nothing to do with being a tough guy or peer pressure, but I cannot tell you that my choice is right for you.

What if I removed myself from the equation?

Only you know the value you put on your own life and what risks you want to take to remain alive.

Now lets try and give a little advice if you have been led to believe that you can take a knife away from someone from 2 miles away with a jumping, spinning, rolling, singing and dancing, left eye lid strike.

This ignorance and misinformation may send you to your grave, as with any others you advise likewise. At the very least you will get cut, so let me give you some advice on the knife and dealing with wounds so you can live to tell your tale.

- Many stab victims thought they had been punched and did not realise they had been stabbed until they saw blood.
- With a very sharp tip, a knife will drive in up to the grip as easy as a hot knife going through butter
- Once the skin is punctured on the chest or abdomen, a knife will slide in with no further force due to the skin acting as an elastic reservoir
- A knife wound can be much deeper than the length of the blade due to the indentation caused by the force of the stab
- Blood flowing out of the body will give a burning sensation
- A slash or stab opening the large arteries in the neck, armpit or groin can cause a fatal haemorrhage in no time at all
- Apply pressure to a wound to stop the flow of blood, breath slowly, deep and rhythmic to delay shock.
- Raise any cut limbs in order to reduce blood pressure
- Close up any chest wound to stop the lungs from collapsing, keep your airway clear and tilt your head back incase you pass out
- For a Stomach wound - lay face down to relieve the pressure

That's just a few of the survival basics to alert you to the real world. There is much more to learn which may be a real lifesaver if the "special technique" fails you...

"Lesley Harrison came within a minute of dying after a burglar stabbed her through the heart with a screwdriver. She was stabbed after confronting Stephen Doyle, a heroin addict in December 1992, he was jailed for 15 years. Her life was saved by a surgeon who plugged the wound with his finger until it could be stitched."

Breaking into your own home

As stupid as it may seem, many of us have had to do it some time in our lives, due to not having our keys. The saddest thing about it is we have all been able to do it relatively easily even through we are not cunning criminals.

So supposing somebody else wanted to break into your home and Lay in wait for you to, to Rape you !

This is why I am concerned about *the security of your home*, I have no concern as to the possibility of you losing your T.V or video from a break in, I am worried about the loss of your liberty **or your life**.

So how are you going to minimise the possibility of a villain laying in wait for you to return home?

Try your hardest to break into your own home, without using your keys. This will show up the weaknesses *so that you can strengthen them*. When you have erased every possibility of an intruder gaining entry and laying in wait, Ask a friend or relative to do the same (with your permission) just to see if they can get in and if they were able to do it without alerting the neighbors, police etc.

Don't forget to take into consideration Different times of the day and night, Different times of the year, Holidays etc., and even consider a criminal approaching your home impersonating a postman, milkman, fast food delivery service, etc.
Make your home impregnable **without your keys** and for your own benefit it may be worth you having a spare set kept with someone **you trust**, because if you lose your keys, how will you get in.

Role play your own abduction

Just like Breaking into your own home, the danger areas of your own abduction must be made known to you. If you can find a time or place that you feel vulnerable to abduction, I'm sure another person would be able to take advantage of this with the greatest of ease.

So minimise the risk and role play your own abduction. It will open your eyes.

Date rape

The World is full of lonely Men and Women who need a partner in their lives. There are many ways relationships are formed naturally, along with alternative methods like Dating agencies, telephone chat lines, National and local news paper adverts, etc.

There is no doubt about it that meeting a stranger through one of these channels can be a traumatic experience. You also have the added threat of some of the people that you meet, being less than genuine in their search for a partner.

The worst cases of this are the adverts containing a recorded message, of the person placing the advert. This system allows us to make direct contact within minutes and a meeting possible within the hour.

The procedure is for you to listen to their message, then have a contact number for them to call you back to arrange a meet.
No harm can come to you over the phone.
Its the meet that involves the threat, if the person is not Genuine.

Let me present you a Big Bad Wolf scenario.

I, as the Big Bad Wolf, want to abuse a single female.

1. I place an advert - ***Lonely Guy wishes to meet female*** etc.
OR
2. You place an advert - ***single female wishes to meet Man*** etc.

Either way we will make telephone contact, I can present myself over the phone to be everything you want me to be.

No matter what you ask, I will be it.

I will find out what you don't like and I will be the complete opposite. The only time you will see through my lies is when we meet, which will never happen on a friendly basis..

I have no intention of meeting you for a date.

I will make the arrangement with you, but view you from a distance. You will be a Lamb going to the Slaughter.

I will now know what you look like, Know you are single, and without you knowing I will follow you home.

We will get to meet sometime in the future when I feel Hungry and come to satisfy my needs to take power and control of you against your will...

You will never know it was connected to the time that you were stood up.

Stalking

Stalking has different degrees, ranging from nuisance to a personal threat. It can be unknown Stalking, were someone becomes infatuated with you and begins to turn up in some of the places you visit, to get that all important glimpse or they may haunt you for life, turning up everywhere , at all times of the day or night, making your life hell. They may even, in extreme cases, threaten to take your life.

I will be the first to admit that I was guilty of the less extreme kind of stalking as a young lad, when I fancied a pretty young girl, but didn't have the courage to approach her directly. As soon as I spotted her with a boyfriend, I called it a day and moved on. No harm was intended. Unfortunately this is not always the case for some others, even if the relationship starts innocently enough.

A stalker can become completely deranged and obsessive, the infatuation taking over his or her mind. The become convinced that the victim desires an intimate relationship with them despite every denial.
The stalker will try to interfere with their victim's life in as many ways as possible, following them, stopping them in the street, phoning them, faxing them, sending presents and flowers etc.
As matters degenerate the presents can turn to threats, the messages can take the form of damage to property of the victim and finally, their personal injury and even death.

"In march 1982 Aurthur Jackson stabbed Raging Bull actress Theresa Saldana 10 times with a 5 inch kitchen knife. She had acted in a film called Defiance, which Jackson believed was his life story, and Theresa Saldana was his girlfreind."

" On 30th march 1981 John Hickney shot Ronald Regan to prove his love to actress Jodie Foster. The whole episode was believed to have been influenced by the film Taxi Driver, where the taxi driver set out to kill the president to prove his love to the young prostitute (played by Jodie Foster)"

" In 1996 a stalker attaching himself to Madonna eventually threatened to cut her throat before being shot by her bodyguard's and later jailed"

But don't believe for one minute that it is just the rich and famous who become victims of stalkers. It can happen to anybody.

Stalking runs very close in line with obsession, the difference being that stalking focuses on seeing someone who is out of reach, whereas an obsession can apply to many things in life.

But what about when mental or physical harm is the result?

" Stalker Anthony Burstow was jailed for three years on charges of inflicting grievous bodily harm through psychiatric damage to work colleague Tracy Sant"

If you are unlucky your perfect partner can become an obsessive stalker if the relationship comes to an end.

You may not even know who your stalker is or what he looks like.

So how do you deal with the situation if you have not got Madonna's cash?

Here are a few tips:-

1. Take out an injunction banning the stalker from making contact or coming near you. You do this exactly as you would in the case of a marriage breakdown, when a male partner is accused of threatening behaviour or violence and needs to be forced to keep away from the former partner. An injunction must have powers of arrest attached to it, without this injunction the Police cannot do much to help.

2. If you are threatened in any way report it to the Police and explain that you are in **fear for your safety** or the safety of your child and go for a charge of **Common Assault** as a minimum, but push for a charge of **Grievous Bodily Harm**.

3. Create a diary to document all the harassment you receive at the hands of the stalker. Include all the incidents, the times and places they occur, what was said and what happened.

4. Make sure as many of your friends and colleagues know what is happening to you and obtain statements from any witnesses who see or hear incidents.

5. Keep all letters, faxes, gifts or messages sent to you, including tapes on answer machines or tapes the stalker may send you.

6. Take photographs of, or film the stalker if you can without putting yourself at risk, or get a friend to.

7. Ask the local crime prevention officer to look at your home security in the light of what is happening to you and ask him to suggest improvements.
8. Do not try to reason with the Stalker. They are not reasonable people and will thrive on the attention you are giving them as you try to reason.

 9. Avoid putting personalised information into your outside rubbish bin such as telephone bills listing phone numbers, work information, clubs you belong to etc. A stalker can easily steal or search through your rubbish to build up a larger database of information about you and will be able to get further into your life.

10. Remember all the other information you have picked up from this book about Scanning, Evaluation, Avoidance and escape, mapping out your routes and leaving messages etc., all of which apply if you find yourself the victim of a Stalker.

Despite all the above safeguards you could still find yourself face to face with an obsessive, demented person who is intent on teaching you a lesson or trying to make you see 'sense', their sense.

The Law and all its worth is of no help to you if you find yourself alone with a crazed stalker intent on making you suffer for not wanting them.

Unfortunately, you will then be in the position of needing to decide if the threat you are facing is Simple, Serious, or Life threatening, as discussed earlier in the book
You must act accordingly.

Crime statistics
Summary of information

Here are some statistics to give you something to think about.
These are the official recorded statistics of the Metropolitan
Police district only. Bear in mind also the fact that these are the
reported offences, who knows how many more go unreported?

1992 -1993	1993-1994	1994-1995
Sexual Offences.		
6,027	6,874	6,820
Rape.		
1,199	1,361	1,410
Indecent Assault (on a female).		
3,368	3,724	3,618
Violence against the person.		
38,359	41,501	42,679

Desensitised

We are a nation who have gradually become desensitised to the reality and horrors that are inflicted to the women and children in our society, purely because it has almost become standard daily news. We are becoming un shockable.

The only way we seem able to get back to becoming sensitive to the horrors that still go on, is when we hear of a few dramatic and horrific occurrences closely linked together.

For this purpose I have included true life cases throughout this book and will now finish off by listing some more for you to read through.

All the sex crimes mentioned within this book are true and have happened within the United Kingdom over the last few years with only one or two reaching back a little further. I have purposely avoided listing Paedeophile assaults with the exception of one, because these warrant a publication on that area alone. Also I have avoided serial killers and the Compton Street murders because There is enough information currently available within the media.

"Seven years ago, Catherine Hall was grabbed by a stranger and forced into his flat, a pair of scissors were pressed into her neck as she was raped. She later escaped by jumping through a window. She landed naked & bruised, on a flat roof two floors below. The rapist was sentenced to 14 years.

"73-year- Vera Laver was rugby-tackled and raped only yards from her house. She died of a stroke brought on by her ordeal."

"A gang of six who raped a woman and threw her into a canal after she told them she could not swim."

"Perry Southall, was stalked and subjected to 200 incidents of harassment by Clarence Morris, who had previously been jailed for six years in 1979 for raping a 15-year-old girl. He had 45 previous convictions for sexual offences and assault."

"A woman was raped and another woman attacked after a gunman tricked his way into her hotel room."

"Patrick Shaw raped an 80 year old woman at knife-point after following her home. He had previously served a jail term for attacking a schoolgirl."

"Paul Cunningham, a former lover of Julia Mason was jailed for five years for throwing a petrol bomb through her window.
Two months earlier Mrs Mason was raped by Ralston Edwards"

"Two 12 year old girls were tied to a tree and raped at knifepoint after being confronted by a hooded attacker. The rapist, threatened to kill his victims as they pushed their bicycles along a path after an afternoon picnic. He ordered both of them to strip, before tying them to a tree with their own shoe laces and making blindfolds from their clothes. The rapist forced the girls to tell them where they lived, in an attempt to persuade them not to report the attack"

"A boy of five hid under his bedclothes as he heard his 60 year old grandmother being raped in the next bedroom by a rapist who broke into the house. For an hour she was sexually assaulted, raped, punched repeatedly and beaten with a belt "She put up a struggle but did not shout out as her grandson was in the house and feared for his safety"

"Kevin Lakeman, had been found guilty of raping two women and trying to rape another 1982. Originally charged with 30 offences, including 12 rapes and 14 attempted rapes. In the first, he held a knife to the throat of a 16 year old girl Then he marched her to woodland where he raped her. His second victim, aged 20, also had a knife held to her throat, before being taken to a nearby playing field and raped..
One of his victims was repeatedly raped at knifepoint and dragged around a park. He grabbed her round the neck from behind warning her not to scream.
His alibi was that he had been with his pregnant girlfriend, Janet Prior, at the time of the three attacks."

"A 16 year old girl walking through woods with her boyfriend was dragged off by a man armed with a handgun and a knife and raped."

"Rapist Darren Whytock, jailed for rape in 1993, returned to his victim's home after being released from prison and attacked her again. He climbed through the bathroom window while she was in her flat with her young son"

"A 21 year old student was so severely attacked that her dental records, DNA test and fingerprint techniques had to be used to get a positive identification. She had been severely beaten about the head, dumped naked and set on fire"

"Two Prostitutes saw Christopher Davies, a client sentenced to 14 years after they brought a private prosecution, believed to be the first of its kind in English law. Both women had been forced to submit to sexual acts at knifepoint while visiting Davies at his bedsit back in 1991 & 1992. The first victim was tied up, then he sat on her chest and held a knife to her throat before raping her. He was found guilty of rape, indecent assault, false imprisonment and assault occasioning actual bodily harm. He had a previous conviction for the attempted kidnapping of a woman who he snatched in the street at knifepoint in 1988 for which he received 12 months in jail."

"Victor Willoughby was given five life sentences for assaults on eight women, however detectives believe that he may have struck more than 100 times, as he stalked women in a year-long series of attacks"

*"Convicted rapist Gavin McGuire was jailed for life for the murder of a 16 year old schoolgirl as she walked home from a pantomime.
Miss Julyan, was punched, kicked, sexually assaulted and strangled with her own blouse. Her naked body was found in a bunker.
McGuire, was previously sentenced to a young offenders' institute for 10 years in 1977 after being convicted of rape, and In 1986 he was jailed for 10 years for attempted rape but was released after six years."*

"A woman told a jury that her self-defence training provided no protection when a Glen Grant broke down her door, burst into her home, beat her almost unconscious and raped her three times.
The 26 year old woman trained in Thai boxing , managed to bloody her attacker's nose but was overpowered and repeatedly punched as she fought to resist him. He grabbed a knife from the kitchen and threatened to kill her if she did not stop screaming. He received five life sentences for violent crimes committed after his release from a secure mental hospital.
In 1984, he became known as the "Beast of Belgravia" when he was convicted of raping two women in their homes, after threatening them with a hammer. He received a 10-year sentence at the Old Bailey on his 16th birthday."

"Paedophile Howard Hughes's was given three life sentences for the murder of seven year old Sophie Hook after abducting her from a tent in her uncle's garden.
Police had been aware of his sexual deviance for 15 years but they had been unable to secure convictions against him because the parents of his young victims were reluctant to allow them to testify.
He had been charged with raping a 14-year-old girl nine years ago and assaulted a seven-year-old boy in 1981, for which he was given a two-year supervision order. Over the years he was interviewed about many allegations which included making indecent suggestions to a four year old and attempted rape of a 15-year-old."

"Leslie Malcolm, 31, confessed to the knifepoint rape of a pregnant 18 year old which he committed only three months after being released 4 years early from his 10 years jail sentence for raping another teenager at knifepoint."

"Richard Whyte was jailed for life after he battered 29-year-old Caroline Williams around the head, stabbed her in the neck, raped and murdered her after breaking into her home in 1994"

"In February 1996, a 12 year old schoolgirl was grabbed from behind, dragged her to nearby waste ground and raped"

"HOODED rapist James McIlroy openly stood outside the homes of his victims threatening that they "would be next" for a period of two years before finaly being caught. His crimes became increasingly uglier and violent, one of his victims were raped and forced to have sexual intercourse on a sofa while she held her three-year-old son."

"In the New Christian Herald, Mrs C Williams, a rape victim, said that for 9 years she has worn a chastity belt made of tempered stainless steel, edged and lined with neoprene and locked by a unique system that uses keys that cannot be copied. She was brutally assaulted and raped 13 years ago by a man she knew. She said that the advice she received from rape crisis counsellors on how to reduce her fear of men had been unhelpful, So too were her self-defence classes."

"Celine Figard, the French student murdered during a Christmas holiday in Britain, had been raped before being strangled and battered to death"

"Claire Hood, 15, was ambushed and sexually assaulted close to her home as she took a short-cut through Cath-Cobb wood.
A 13-year-old girl from the same school as Claire was also attacked in a separate incident when walking home through the grounds of a derelict house when she was beaten over the head by a man with a wooden club."

"Rachael Lean, an 18 year old student was found stabbed to death in woods She died from multiple stab wounds."

"Nicola wilson tourtured and burned a teenage girl on her face, eyelids, and body with a cigarette and repeatedly beat her. She also acted as ringleader whilst her boyfriend Johny Wilson and other gang member Stephen Dixon took it in turns to rape her. Other members of the gang tried to force the vicyin to drink urine."

196

Conclusion

I hope you have found this book educational and informative.

For me to have included everything that I wanted to cover connected with female self protection, would have taken more time and pages than I have available.
Taking into account the many reports of violence against women in just the last few years alone, I decided that this book should not be postponed any longer. If a reading of this book helps just one woman to deal with or to avoid male abuse or violence over the next year, my decision to write this book will have been right.

Sadly, no matter how far I search or how deeply I journey into the area of female self protection, I can only tell it from the male perspective. I can never fully experience the effect that male abuse has had on the feelings, attitudes and emotions of a woman who has suffered at the hands of a male.
I can only do my best to support you and try to see things from your perspective. However this book will give you a good starting point from which to add or delete areas that are relevant to your safety.

Now you have something to be working with, I can work on other related matters by releasing further publications, videos, and conducting seminar's
Over time, through trial and error, sharing information, and some fine tuning, we will gradually be making progress in our efforts to help you avoid and deal with future threat.

" Train, as you live, in both mind and body "

Jamie

Thank you to all my friends within the New Breed training system for their help with the photographs, plus their dedication and promotion of practical Self Protection.

New Breed are:-
Bob Wallace, Micky Byrne, Steve Kemp, Tony Wiggins, Andy Landers, Otis Samuels, Martin Dibben, Marc Kaylor, Pete West, Micky & Jacky Neale, Vickie Moss, Brian Flint, Gary Wilson.
Special thanks also to my friend Pat O'Malley for the hundreds of hours we have spent together training and philosophising

My respects also go out to my friend Kevin Fox. The most dedicated, respectful, and toughest individual I have ever known, for the years we have spent together exchanging techniques & ideas within training, plus our time in action within the ugliest arena's possible, entrusting our lives to each other and defying deaths door on many occasions..

This book has taken 2 years of long lonely solitude nights with nothing more than four walls for company.

Has it all been worthwhile ?

I think so !

" The best form of revenge is Success "